PO PAI MO

THE SEARCH FOR WHITE BUFFALO WOMAN

D0869911

PO PAI MO

THE SEARCH FOR WHITE BUFFALO WOMAN

ROBERT BOISSIERE

Sunstone Press
Santa Fe, New Mexico

FIRST EDITION. Printed in the United States of America.

Library of Congress Cataloging in Publication Data:

Boissiere, Robert, 1914 –   .
      Po Pai Mo. The search for white buffalo woman

      1. White Buffalo Woman. 2. Taos Indians—Biography. 3. Boissiere, Robert, 1914·   . 4. Indianists—
Biography. 5. Taos Indians—Social life and customs. 6. Hopi Indians—Social life and customs. I. Title.
E99.T2B64   1983   970.004'97 (B)   83–4668

ISBN: 0-86534-042-2

Published in 1983 by SUNSTONE PRESS / Post Office Box 2321 / Santa Fe, New Mexico 87501 / USA

TABLE OF CONTENTS

DEDICATION

ACKNOWLEDGEMENTS

This book is dedicated to my dear and devoted wife.

I would like to acknowledge the memory of the great men who have urged me forward in my quest for White Buffalo Woman:

Professor LeComte du Nouy, biophysician, researcher, Rockefeller Institute associate member, well-known author;

Father Teilhard de Chardin, discoverer of Sinopithecus (Peking man) paleontologist, philosopher and writer;

Paul Coze, philosopher, writer, great friend of the Southwest Indian tribes;

Dr. Frederick Hodge, Director of California Southwest Museum.

Long before Christopher Columbus' discovery of the western continents, the Indian-American had won this land from nature and had achieved an harmonious relation with the bountiful environment it offered. The gift of the Indian—spiritual and material—to America has been wondrous and rich. Destiny has marked the Rio Grande valley as the meeting ground of the Anglo-american and the Hispano-american with the original Indian-american. Here one day will arise a new Americanism from the intermingling of these three great currents of American culture.

REGINALD
FISHER

AUTHOR'S NOTE

This is the true story of my search for White Buffalo Woman and my life with Po Pai Mo whom I truly believe was sent to guide me on this quest.

Both in Europe and here in America, I had searched and prayed for years that I would be permitted to find the path which leads to a true understanding of life—my own, in particular.

The story which follows is the true account of the final chapter of this search when, with immense gratitude, I began to realize that my prayers had been answered.

Through a long process that required my utmost attention, a beautiful woman took me by the hand, my own white buffalo woman, to lead me to the spirit of the one who, long ago, had come to lovingly guide her chosen people, the Indians of the Americas, along with all the people of the earth, toward a true understanding of their presence on the planet.

Black Elk, spiritual leader of the Oglala Sioux told John G. Neihardt, his narrator, how his people received the gift of the Sacred Pipe Ceremony from White Buffalo Woman.

He says, "It is the story of all life that is holy and is good to tell. It is not the tale of a great hunter or of a great warrior...a very long time ago...it is the story of a very sacred woman who wore a fine white buckskin dress. Her hair was very long. She was young and very beautiful.

"'You shall go home,' she said, 'and tell your people that I am coming and that a big tepee shall be built for me in the center of the nation.' And as she sang, there came from her mouth a white cloud that was good to smell. Then she gave to the chief a pipe with a bison calf carved on one side with twelve eagle feathers hanging from the stem.

"'Behold,' she said, 'with this you shall multiply and be a good nation. Nothing but good shall come from it.' As she went out of the tepee, suddenly it was a white bison galloping away and snorting, and soon it was gone.

"To the Indians, she is known as White Buffalo Woman."

1 AMERICA

Through the window of the transatlantic Constellation I could see the outlines of the skyscrapers of Manhattan. The trip from Lisbon had been pleasant though tiresome, many long hours in the air. I thought of Lindbergh alone in his small plane crossing the same huge gulf between clouds and threatening waves. As a child of thirteen, I saw his plane passing over our house near Paris on a beautiful morning as all of France acclaimed him as the great hero of "outre atlantique."

I drifted through these long hours between imagination, dream and memory. Now seeing America at last, one of the great moments of my life was near at hand. If it had not been for an American Consul friend who insisted that post-war America was the only land of opportunity left, I might have drifted toward the jungles of Brazil and relocated there.

After the liberation by the Allied forces, France was in turmoil, not only from a physical reconstruction standpoint, but after four years of German occupation the country was politically, socially and economically in a state of shock. I had served as well as I could and, in the end, all my possessions — house, furniture, mementos — had been reduced to ashes.

It was my American stepfather who had given me the dream, who had nurtured the desire to know his country. But before I get back to my "Manhattan transfer," I should explain a few things. First, we had an old family friend who was the American Consul in Lisbon and it was through him I learned that the French immigration quota was not as crowded there as it was in Paris. So I made up my mind this was the best route out.

During the war, my stepfather had stayed the whole length of the occupation in the non-occupied zone south of the Loire River because he did not want to risk going to a concentration camp in the German-occupied zone where Paris was. At that time I hid a full year with the Basques, the "Esqualdunas" as they called themselves, running the risk of deportation after escaping from my "stalag" in September 1941.

That year in the Pyrenees with the incredible mountain people, doing contraband with them at times over the Spanish border, I realized some great change was in store for me, some destiny of which I was unaware. Without the confidence this feeling brought about, I might never have gone on to Lisbon and from there to America. Something convinced me of that when I experienced an incredible mystical circumstance during my stay with the Esqualdunas way above Saint Jean Pied de Port, high in the Pyrenees. Even though I am back-tracking, I must relate what happened—for the moment, Portugal and Manhattan can wait.

One Sunday morning I sensed a great need to climb a nearby mountain to experience solitude and prayer. I often did that. After bicycling several kilometers, I chose a rocky peak which seemed suitable for my ascent. It happened as I was saying a rosary on top of this jagged promontory which thrust itself straight at the sky. I felt a presence behind me. The awful sensation of an unknown power, cold as the ice mountain I sat on. (There is a mental process which I learned later called locution, described by visionaries as consisting of "hearing" words directly with the mind without going through the normal auditory channel. In other words, the mind "knows" although no sound has occurred.) The presence near me let me know that my desires could become a reality if I would surrender to him, or rather It. I identified the presence since as an evil

13

force, a dimension of the Devil. Brandishing my rosary high over my head, I exclaimed in a loud voice, "I don't need you, I have this." Then I shook all over with an incredibly loud laugh echoing from mountain top to mountain top all around me. Instantly, the presence vanished and I began my vertical descent down the mountain. Without knowing it at first—as if in a dream state—I took leaps that must have been twenty or more feet each, and in this way, I plummeted down the mountain weightless and free. Such a thing is hard to believe—it was certainly hard for me to grasp, but only after it was over. While I did it, I was practically unaware of anything except the sensation of complete liberation, a feeling which continued from that day forward.

Several months later, my father met me in Bayonne, the French Basque capital of Southern France. He brought my wife with him and a few hours later, we crossed the Spanish border. We spent the first night in the fortified town of Burgos. The next day we crossed into Portugal through one of the most arid but beautiful countrysides I had ever seen.

After finding an apartment for my wife and me in downtown Lisbon and after spending a few weeks with us discovering the loveliness of Portugal, my father returned to France. However, before leaving he gave me a letter of introduction to the Cardinal of Lisbon from Monsignor Verdier, Cardinal of Paris. My father knew the Cardinal was the *Eminence Grise*, power behind the scenes, of Portugal's President Salazar. And my father never left anything to chance; he knew in leaving us behind that if we were to need any kind of protection, we could secure it that way. It just so happened that the kind of protection that this letter offered me was of a very different nature.

I met the Cardinal at his palace; he was a charming man who spoke meticulous French and I somehow felt what it must have been like to sit before the presence of Cardinal de Richelieu or Mazarin, *Eminence Grises* of splendors past.

What this led to was a later meeting with the Mother Superior of the French order of the Sisters Dorothys. In conversation with the Cardinal, I mentioned my interest in Fatima. The next thing I knew he had arranged for me to visit the convent where Lucia, the eldest of the three visionaries of Fatima, had become a nun. If you are not familiar with what occurred on October 13, 1917, I will explain it.

Three little shepherds, Lucia, Jacinta and Francisco, had visions of a heavenly being whom they called the "beautiful lady." They were punished and ostracized for their vision and, in their despair, they asked their heavenly friend to show the disbelieving multitudes an irrefutable sign of truth.

On that day, October 13, 1917, before a crowd of nearly 60,000 people, what has been later called "the miracle of the sun" took place. For a brief moment around noon, the sun shone silvery in the sky and appeared to descend down in a spiral upon the crowd. This lasted perhaps forty seconds during which time people prayed and fell to the ground. The shepherds' "beautiful lady" kept her word.

I learned more of these events of 1917 through Sister Eugenie Gilbert who knew Lucia as a nun. In this way, I was able to get first hand information. In fact, later that year, while in meditation in one of Lisbon's churches, and through the same process of locution, I learned it was time for me to go to Fatima myself to seek details of the visitations.

I left the next morning via an overcrowded small bus, the only mode of transportation available to me to go to this little mountain village high in the golden hills of Portugal. It was there the following day, after spending a whole night on my knees with peasants and shepherds, that I witnessed my own miracle of the sun: surrounded by a corona of rainbow colors, the sun appeared at midday as I had never seen it before nor since.

I think a little more background on myself at this point should be given so you may better understand what follows. If my story seems to jump around, I apologize. But my life, rich and full, varied and blessed, has not always behaved in an orderly fashion. Therefore, my life story will take its own turns.

I was born in Paris at the beginning of World War I to parents who were part of Paris' *bourgeoisie,* what in America would be called upper class. I never knew my father because he was killed in the first month of the Great War, trying to stop the same German invasion that I faced twenty-five years later. Luckier than he, I escaped with only a few scratches after eighteen months in captivity. But Sister Fate is as unpredictable as my method of writing. Let me explain.

One dark evening a column of tanks and trucks was progressing toward the front in Belgium when a wave of stuckas dived on us before we had time to jump from our trucks. I was lucky. The small town in which we were caught, Charleroi, was the very place my father was killed twenty-five years earlier, doing exactly what I was doing: trying ineffectively to stop the invaders at the historic corridor of their invasion, the Belgian countryside.

Like almost all of the French army in June 1940, I was taken prisoner; I managed to escape unscathed eighteen months later. I might never have contemplated breaking away from a prison camp, guarded by hundreds of German soldiers including a company of SS, if I had not been singled out as a possible hostage.

The prisoners had organized a system by which letters could be sent to their families since the camp was in the still-French-occupied territories. Every day one prisoner was designated to take the stack of letters to the fence where our guardians let us get cigarettes from villagers, usually girls. During the trade, we played the game of slip-the-letters-without-attracting-attention.

I don't know if the Germans observed us but one day when it was my turn and I had, perhaps, forty letters to pass on, they arrested me. Thrown into isolation in the SS quarters, I was told that I would be executed in the morning. I spent the entire night in prayer. In the morning, with almost no preliminaries, they released me. I could hardly believe it—I was free again. Or at least I was free within the confines of the camp. Best of all, I was still alive, the only real freedom one can depend on.

A month later, after a lot of secret talks with my friend, a cyclist champion, we planned an escape. Better said than done, of course, but one foggy morning when it was so dense you could hardly see twenty feet in front of your nose, we knew the time had come.

The Germans used to operate a grain silo in the camp. Between it and the double fence circling the camp were the latrines.

We figured out that someone could slip from behind them and get to the fence without being spotted from the silo. We had also observed that the German patrol between the double fences would give us exactly seven mintues to dig under it.

So we both asked to go to the john and, at first, no suspicion was aroused. On our knees, we slipped toward the fence, dug under the first one using our bare hands, then under the second. Then we raced toward the bushes. What we did not know was that the Germans had cleared almost a hundred feet of forest,. But the fog enabled us to reach cover safely and we threw ourselves on our bellies behind some bushes and lay very still. A German patrol came along and did not notice the holes we had made.

We waited till nightfall to move toward the river, the border between the two zones. That night we took refuge in a peasant cottage and it was there we heard sirens. They knew we were missing and we knew they would comb the countryside for us.

Early in the morning, the lady of the house took us to the river disguised as well-to-do fishermen. She knew when the horse patrols would move along the river. My fishing pole shook when the Germans passed behind us studying our attire.

"Bien mes gars, allez y!"

This wonderful French farm lady urged us to run for it, risking her own life in the process.

Rushing through the waters, the current slowing our progress, we crawled and ran and swam the boundary line to freedom.

After that I had to live under a false identity provided by the French authorities for the duration of the German occupation. The terms of the armistice treaty were explicit: all escaped prisoners were to be returned to the German authorities.

I had plenty of time to reflect on the reasons which led to the fall of France. For me, like most of my countrymen, the shock of the military defeat and the occupation of our country by enemy forces was devastating, physically, emotionally and every other way.

Twenty-five years of bad politics and weak policies toward Germany had given Nazi-ism its stranglehold. France was not equipped to resist the well-organized thrust and the invaders did not stop at the gates of Paris as they had in my father's time, 1914, but they entered the capital and lived as conquerors for almost four years.

So now I hope I have supplied a few more reasons why I learned to trust my heart and my inner-eye at such an early age. During the war all of our family possesions were destroyed in the advance of the Allied forces. The war itself actually transformed me. In looking back, even now as I write this, a wave of nostalgia for pre-war Paris sweeps over me. The end of a working day when the offices emptied themselves of the *midinettes*, office workers spilling their numbers on the *Grand Boulevards* in search of a quiet cafe to enjoy a Pernod or a Cinzano at the end of the day. Christmas time with its smell of roasted chestnuts wafting from every street corner, people eating oysters on the half-shell in the street. But all of this fades as it must now, as it did then.

I return to our story and to the window of the huge bird carrying my wife and me across the Atlantic. I see the Statue of Liberty. Tipping its wings to land, the plane cuts above the skyscrapers of the city of New York. Today it seems a dream —or is there any difference? Is the passage of time irrelevant? Is reality merely the end result of all our dreams? Or another state altogether? We pass from one thing to another, awake or asleep and it is all one: the writing, the living, the remembering.

New York was to be only a step in the reassessment of our lives. Because I had contacts in California through my stepfather, we headed for the Pearl of the Pacific, land of sun, opportunities, a new life. San Francisco, here we come!

The train ride across the continent was something I will never forget: Chicago, the Great Salt Lake, the Rockies. It was our own conquest of the West a hundred and fifty years after the gold rush.

In a month's time after our arrival, we had a deposit on a house and I had a job. It was no dream anymore, but commuting every morning to work, meeting the bills, thinking of having our children sent to us. At that time they were with their grandmother in Paris.

My English was not much yet, but it was improving as I

went from the basement of the only real French department store in San Francisco to the first floor selling men's apparel and finally to managing the French book shop.

The Verdier family who owned the store had been long friends of my family, but it was up to me to make a success for myself and I did. French atmosphere, beautiful girls, latest fashions —I fit right in. I bridged Paris, my early love, to my new home on the Pacific coast.

Peace and security slowly replaced the turbulence that the war years had installed in my psyche. I was beginning to evaluate the traumas that my mind, my body and my soul had been laminated by.

This reassessment within took many forms. I was writing a lot, still in French. The "journal of a despaired man" I called it. It was, indeed, out of desperation that I wrote those pages full of intimate turmoil, questions about myself, and life in general. The inner turmoil following the war, the occupation, the loss of my homeland was indescribable.

A storm was taking place within me, leading me to another storm outside myself in my life. It seemed that my passionate inner self was about to explode. Although I had the peace and comfort I had dreamed about in the Nazi camp, I now felt saddened by it, not overjoyed but weighed down, burdened by my own release.

And the beautiful women who had become part of my everyday life at work led to the sensual world I had tried to denounce. In quiet desperation, I fell in love with a Tahitian beauty who took me, in spirit, to the white beaches of her native island. Many passionate afternoons were spent on those brilliant imaginary shores that my countryman, Gauguin, had painted so well that I could step into them.

The statuesque beauty of Paquita, true daughter of her Aztec ancestors, took hold of my imagination. I cannot forget the hours of reveries we spent together in our favored lounge or strolling the beaches of San Francisco at sunset.

Janine was modelling incredible fashions straight from Paris. Her slender body would parade Lanvin or Dior through my department two, three times a day. Flirting was part of the job, I suppose. Resting her langorous body on the shelves where Henry Miller's *Tropique du Cancer* or Alexis Carrel's *L'Homme Cet Inconnu* were displayed was enough for what was left of unused passion to career out of bounds. Lunches in the private booths of Chinese restaurants in Chinatown ushered us, enraptured, out into the busy streets. Later a Pacific sunset would cap the day. Janine was as passionate as I was and the persistent storm in my life broke all conventional and moral bonds that had brought me safely through the war. Before I knew it, my marriage was on the rocks. Lise and I—married twelve years, our marriage having taken place on the eve of World War II—were suddenly estranged in a foreign land. Only six months had elapsed from the time of our honeymoon to the day I was in the trenches. We had been through so much together, two lovely children who were now living with us, peace—at last—and now, what appeared to be ruination.

This backlash hit me with shock after shock. All that had been bottled up before the war played havoc with my conscious mind. It was only in dream that the harmony was restored. I know it often works the opposite way, with the dream being agonized and the conscious life controlled, but in me it was the reverse.

One dream, in particular, kept recurring night after night. I was an eagle flying high in the sky. Below me was a checkerboard of what appeared to be a destroyed city, the empty cubicles of the demolished houses.

I would land at the foot of a two-story square tower leaning on a cliff. Entering through a small door at the bottom of the tower, I would climb inside and find a ladder opening to a roof. There, on a flat plateau, the ruins of an ancient city lay in front of me—silence and beauty, the end of all disharmony.

I felt that this dream held the key to events ahead of me in my life. It left me pensive, decisively sure that an understanding of it was of great importance. Intuition proved correct.

But in the meantime, I met writers, intellectuals at my French book shop at the store. I entered intro correspondence with several of them and two in particular were to influence my life on a grand scale. They became my mentors.

Pierre LeComte Du Nouy was the major influence, leading me not only to a complete reversal of my troubled life, but giving me a key to open the door that I knew was waiting to be opened. He was a research biologist and Rockefeller Institute member most known for his bestseller *Human Destiny*, a leading researcher of the modern evolutionist movement and Du Nouy was readily available to me through his kind and detailed letters, answering questions and sharing thoughts whenever I wrote to him.

My other teacher was Pierre Teilhard de Chardin, best known for his discovery of the Pekinese man (Sinanthropus) in China, writer of many books including *The Phenomenon of Man.* Father Teilhard and I entered into a great *epistolaire* relationship. I am grateful and proud that he took the time to correct two of my early essays.

Pierre LeComte Du Nouy died in New York. His wife Mary wrote to me giving me the sad news along with a significant piece of information: He had told her he wished that I would help her sort some of his private notes and papers in his laboratory situated on their estate in Altadena, California.

Somehow, without fully understanding the incredible meaning of it all, I felt extremely honored and very anxious to help Mary LeComte Du Nouy execute the wish of the master.

2 HOPI

I left San Francisco International Airport on January 7, 1948, a date I shall never forget.

Some people do actually feel a momentous event is about to change their lives; in my case, I did.

It began as I was glancing at the usual magazines handed to passengers in such flights. An article in *Desert Magazine* attracted my attention immediately. Paul Coze, the author, was an art teacher, lecturer, writer, philosopher and had been an advisor for the motion picture, *The Razor's Edge*. What interested me about him was his qualification as one of the best authorities on Indians of the Southwest. The fact he was also French gave me cause to want to meet him.

In my childhood, I fantasized (as many of us have done) about being an Indian brave. I can remember a strange longing to locate the "people" who would one day recognize me as one of them. I used the sprawling roots of a majestic elm tree as my tepee; I was nine years old. At Christmas, my request was for a Sioux costume, bonnet and all. I wore it to a rag, having it on day in and day out.

Paul Coze would make sense of all of this, I thought, and possibly help me to better understand my dream. I went to a telephone booth as soon as I reached the Los Angeles airport.

"I am a complete stranger," I told him. "I just read the article in *Desert Magazine*. Could I talk to you about it?. . ."

His French was perfect. "Certainly, why not have dinner at my place at eight. Au revoir!"

I couldn't believe it! In a matter of hours, I was led on a brand new road, far from the one I had followed since I had come to America. It felt right though, I could tell.

The way it came about couldn't have been better. I would be able to spend the whole day with Mrs. Du Nouy as planned and meet in the evening with Paul Coze.

Going through my teacher's notes, in his spacious bureau and private laboratory, was a unique experience I shall never forget. Mrs. Du Nouy spoke some French, but I felt happy to help when the intricacies of the French language became too much for her.

The mansion sat in the midst of eighty acres of avocado

trees, a lovely place in the southern California sun. We had a delightful lunch, during which Mrs. Du Nouy recalled memories of the great researcher, scientist and writer.

Human Destiny had been published solely in French, then, and she gave me one of her last copies. I have read it many times. Her goal was to translate it for publication in this country and the professor's notes were to help her to do it.

The American edition was on the best seller list for five years.

Paul Coze and Leslie in a great discussion.

"Why are you so interested in Indians?" — Paul Coze's first question after I rang his bell at exactly eight p.m. Tall and slender, in his early forties, with prominent cheek bones and a sharp nose, his gaunt appearance and olive complexion gave him the aura of a Plains Indian.

Actually, he was born in Syria, from a French father and a Russian duchess mother. He looked distinguished, a noble tall figure and as I learned later, an amazing scholar.

His question took me by surprise, but since he had zeroed in on the precise reason for my being there, I gave him my best answer — "I've never felt at home in my own culture."

"I never did either," he said.

24

At once I had a friend!

"As a kid, playing Indian was a way to act out my fantasy, to withdraw, to escape the inescapable reality. I read a lot about Indian life," I added.

"Many a French kid does that," he said, trying to see if I were truly sincere."

"Perhaps. But in my case, I identified with it as if I had an Indian inside me who couldn't get out."

Now Paul felt I was telling the truth. "Let's eat," he said amiably. "We can talk more about all this at the table."

I knew he believed me.

"I'm sure I don't have to ask if you like French cooking," he said smiling. "As for me, it is more than a hobby; I love to cook."

"Soupe al'onion.

"Rognons d'agneau aux champignons.

"Salade de Poireaux.

"Camembert."

His menu revealed an unusual man. You would not find such a French assortment of dishes in a typical French restaurant in America. This was authentically French.

"I have a great Bordeaux rouge," he said with that intended smile, placing his right thumb against his index finger in typical French fashion for a gourmand appreciative of fine things. "I want to know what you think."

Silence was *de rigueur* for a time as we tasted his delightful cuisine.

"Do you have any idea what to look for...any special characteristics of Indian people you are looking for?"

"Yes, I do," I told him. "They are a people of peace, set in the old ways. More than that I don't know."

Without hesitation, he answered, "The Hopis of Arizona. They live on high mesas several hundred feet above the desert floor. They are farmers. They never pledge allegiance to any power other than their own. A very proud but also very humble people."

It was close to dawn when I left the home of Paul Coze. Floating in my mind were the mementos of his own search:

kachina dolls, old bows, beaded moccasins. We talked mainly about what he knew of Indian cultures, as well as our own: French, American, the West.

In one evening, my quest for the people I had blindly searched for during an entire lifetime was revealed. Best of all, Paul Coze had asked me to join a party he had organized for his students the coming summer. I was to meet them in Flagstaff for the July 4th All Indian Pow Wow, and leave from there for the Hopi mesas. I could hardly believe all of this. In his own funny way, always conscious of the practical and the economic, Paul had asked me to serve as butler and cook for the trip — it would pay my way! Naturally I accepted with enthusiasm.

I don't know if I realized it then, but my whole life was making a complete turnaround, so drastic, in fact, that it would never be the same. All in one day! The months, years ahead, would give sense to it all, and as far as the present was concerned — I would be watching my dreams become reality, a reality created of pure trust in the heart, in the intuitive faculties of my being.

Squeezed out of my present environment, I began to see France, the war, San Francisco, my family troubles as the antechamber of what was going to be, leading to more dramas, more hard times, more heartaches, but now there was a feeling of growth. Expanding as weeks, months and when dream and reality merge, a true sense of happiness is born. My errors of the past would not be errors anymore; they would be milestones upon which I would walk into the future.

It was not easy to make my family and my employer realize that I needed a sabbatical. I had the clear feeling, though, that my mental balance depended upon it, and this gave me the strength to convince others.

The Indian Pow Wow of 1948 was a beginning. Fifty different tribes, possibly more, gathered in Flagstaff, bringing the best dancers, singers and warriors. I made some beautiful color slides during my stay.

In the evening, strolling the Indian camp with Paul, I got my first opportunity to meet many different kinds of Indians face to face. Paul knew just about everyone from having been on the panel of dance judges over the years. A strong smell of fry bread, roasting green corn, potatoes and chili spiced the evening air. It was wonderful, the enchantment of the moment, a feeling of permanence.

We went·from tent to tepee, shaking hands, exchanging smiles. A brand new experience was making its way into my life, for weeks I would not really grasp the meaning of it, but I had already given in to a deeper trust to the knowledge of feeling instead of thinking.

It was a Tuesday morning, I recall, when Paul stuffed the 1930 Buick convertible with the necessary supplies for the trip to Hopi country. In went the seven of us. What a car that Buick was, an enormous remnant of a past era. Two windshields: one in the middle stood on a retractable hood which protected us from sand and wind.

Paul had warned us the trails in the desert could be treacherous, especially if it had rained. There were no good roads to Hopi in those days; the sand trails were washouts in hard rain.

I was unprepared, I must confess, to face the immensity of the desert. Its magnificence hit me like a thunderbolt, like the first time I heard the Valkyrie of Wagner in the Paris Opera House.

A fantasia of forms and colors at every turn; sand trails taking me away from the comfortable linear world I had know for thirty-five years, taking me to a dimension of greater certainty, greater unknown.

Paul had chosen a paradise for his art students — pinks, greys, mauves, fiery reds. years later, observing color pictures of the planet Mars, I was reminded of some of the things I saw on that first trip to Hopi.

Halfway to our destination — the Hopi village of Oraibi, after six or seven hours of desert driving — what we dreaded most confronted us: a large pool of water too big to go around completely blocked our way. A cloudburst an hour or so before had done it and I could see Paul was more than a little worried. To wait until it dried would involve hours; attempting to cross might bog us down forever.

After talking it over with all of us, Paul decided to cross…

almost at once the sand gave way underneath all that weight and we were stuck in the mud for good. What happened after is hard to describe: hours of cutting bushes, hunkered down in the muddy water putting branches under the wheels, sweating furiously, soaked to the bone in mud and sweat.

Brown from head to toe, we managed, at last, to lay a path for the car. In a burst of churning wheels, mud and water spraying us while we were praying, Paul somehow got the car to the other side.

New Oraibi was a welcome sight at sunset when the spattered Buick pulled up next to the "Lorenzo Hubbell Trading Post."

Hubbell was one of the most respected Indian traders of his day, following a century-old reputation founded by his grandfather. He and Paul were good friends; Lorenzo opened his home to all the students, a courtesy very Southwestern in those days. The place was more of a museum than a home, with every kind of collectible and artifact on display. Here were some of the finest examples of Indian art in the Southwest.

On top of the cliffs, in front of which New Oraibi stood, was Old Oraibi, reputed to be the oldest inhabited community in North America.

My commitment to Paul to be "cook and butler," took a lot of my time during the week that we spent in the Lorenzo house, but not to the point of keeping me from being entranced with my first contact with the land and its people.

Cooking, thus far, had not been my strong point, but no one complained. I kept the place meticulously clean, inspecting the myriads of Indian paintings and relics as I went about my work. The old beaded vest of a Cheyenne warrior hung next to a Remington original, priceless kachina dolls everywhere, shields, bows, arrows, the works.

Paul kept his students on the go all the time. He possessed a boundless vitality which some of the young girls had a hard time coping with. Whenever I could, I took photographs, some of which are included in my narrative. I would climb the mesa behind the village before sunrise when everyone was still asleep. Filling my lungs with that special scent of the desert when the sky moves from darkness of night to greys, pinks, blues of a new day.

Now, some forty years later, these rich and delicate moments have an intimacy with the land and the plants of the Hopi desert that is so strong that I feel it must have happened yesterday. I did not know it then, but I was simply falling in love with the oldest and most rapturous of all mysteries.

Some ten centuries before me, small groups of Anasazis who had emigrated from all four directions — Mesa Verde, Hovenweep, Chaco Canyon, Casas Grandes, perhaps even more south from the land of the Aztecs and the Mayas — had discovered as I did, that what is now Hopi radiates a subtle kind of energy, a source of special power. It was, therefore, destined to harbor a very special kind of people.

I was to discover this firsthand when Paul took me with him to visit his old friend and *kikmongwi* (chief) of the most ancient of all the villages, Old Oraibi. Chief Tawakwaptiwa was then in his late seventies. He received us crosslegged on the dirt floor of a rather small and totally bare room, his wife sitting in the same position next to him. According to Hopi custom, she got up to serve us a cup of coffee and Hopi bread. The old chief told us of a life of peaceful but active resistance to the ways of the white intruders who constantly threatened to obliterate the "sacred Hopi way."

Never will I forget this first meeting with such a strong defender of the ways of his people. The message was clear, as it is still today: "We came here to find peace a long, long time ago; why not leave us in peace..."

I could feel something happening within me, a new response to what I saw and felt. After hours of reflection, I figured out what caused the feeling. Perhaps, for the first time in my life, the dream, the fantasy, all that realm of thinking from the back of my mind and from the bottom of my childhood, was emerging as visual, audible, tangible reality. It was, in a way, as I explained it to myself, the blending of the supernatural and the natural in the same unique experience in the level measuring of the great expanse of the desert. It would not be long before proof of this was upon me; I could sense it.

Hopi was the new dimension, the dream of the soaring eagle.

It took almost three more days for Paul's students to sketch and paint what they wanted to record of New Oraibi, leaving their canvasses to be finished when they went back to their

The Eagle tied to a log on the roof.

respective homes in the *civilized* world.

Ahead of us lay the other villages of Second and First Mesa: Shipaulovi, Shongopavi, Mishongnovi, Walpi, Sichomovi and Hano. We left early for Second Mesa and, still tired from all my chores, I fell asleep in the back seat of Paul's Buick. Sleeping, I didn't realize when he stopped the car on top of a ridge to show his students the astonishingly beautiful sight the village of Shipaulovi presents to the eyes, like an old fortress standing on an inaccessible rock springing out of the desert floor.

I suppose everyone respected my need to sleep that morning because no one awakened me for this feast of the eyes. However, in that deep hypnotic sleep I had fallen into, I was seeing the castle-like structure on top of the rocky piton!

When I woke up and was confronted by it a second time, I knew the unconscious and the conscious had become one at last. What a fantastic way to receive the sign I had been waiting for!

This was the spiritual home it had taken me a lifetime to reach.

From the vantage point where we were standing, down a steep grade and up again on a rocky incline, we left the heavy Buick on a ledge just below the Indian village. Standing right above, Shipaulovi looked like a medieval castle abandoned by the Crusaders. The last part of the incline could not have been mastered by the Buick. On foot it was a torturous climb.

We emerged finally on a small courtyard of solid rock around which the Hopi stone houses were standing like dominos on a checkerboard.

The view was breathtaking, reaching three hundred sixty degrees toward the horizon, perhaps sixty or seventy miles.

Paul felt right at home. He knocked on the first door he came to. I was breathing hard. He motioned us in, and then came a moment in time where everything stood still. The opening door I had seen many times with the eyes of my inner vision.

We entered a large room which was the whole house. Whitewashed and spotless, a fresh odor of cleanliness struck me as something I had never smelled before; it was the natural white dirt the Indians had dug in special places to use as paint for their walls. It smells of the earth itself.

There was practically no furniture except for a small wood-stove, two or three cupboards and a couple of low small benches. Everything was extremely simple, beautiful in its simplicity.

I recognized both the man and his wife immediately — Paul had introduced us in Flagstaff, perhaps knowingly, knowing him.

Leslie Koyawena and his wife Alta were a very handsome couple. In his younger days Leslie's face seemed carved from red standstone the Sioux use in making peace pipes. His piercing dark brown eyes danced brightly. His long curved nose made him look like an Inca.

Sitting on one of the benches, Leslie was working on a donkey saddle that must have been a hundred years old.

One thing struck me about him: the grin on his face. All the other Indians I had met looked serious. Not Leslie, he was grinning all the time!

A bright yellow shirt and turquoise necklace were in sharp

31

contrast to the copper of his skin. The polished turquoise stones hanging from his ear lobes framed his face, along with a bright red bandanna all Hopi men wear around their heads. He was a very handsome man, perhaps forty years old at the time.

Opposite him, working on a Hopi basket made in the shape of a plate and called a plaque, his wife was dressed in the ceremonial black manta that the women and girls wore. Wide

Leslie in front of the house in Shipaulovi. The room on the roof was my quarters.

green and red sash tied around her waist, bare feet, Alta had her hair tied "the married-woman way," two fat sausage strands on each side of the face. In contrast to her husband, Alta's beautiful face was much fuller and fairer than Leslie's with a compassionate smile that made her look like a madonna.

I learned that the plaque she was making was made of woven and coiled yucca strips, designed for a Hopi wedding, serving as a present for the bride's family. That one had a Hopi sun symbol on the four cardinal points, a cross.

After a while, Paul gave us a tour of the tiny stone-built village perched on its rocky pinnacle as if it were the highest point on the planet. Like a lighthouse, Shipaulovi stands above the desert to light the way for lost ships of which I was one.

There were perhaps twenty houses built together, with three or four kivas dug into the solid rock upon which the village was built. Shipaulovi was and is the smallest of all the Hopi villages.

Paul took me outside for a short while. He wanted to talk to me.

"We cannot spend any more time, here," he said, his eyes looking straight into mine. "We have to go on with our trip as planned."

I knew what he was driving at. "If you want to leave the party now," he said, softening, "you know it is all right with me."

He knew my answer. He had known it ever since I met him in Pasadena; he had been faithful to the promise he made then.

"I'd like to stay, Paul, you know that."

Our eyes were moist. Each of us knew what this meant.

*   *   *

The days, weeks, months that followed bringing joys, hardships, anticipations, made my everyday life on top of the lighthouse of the desert a beautiful solitary happening in a world composed only of a few dozen people. It was a tale more lively to me than *A Thousand and One Nights* or *The Light in the Forest*, Rudyard Kipling adventures or J.W. Schultz' *Life Among the Cheyennes*.

I relived some of the accounts I had read of early explorers or Spanish accounts on their first seeing the new world.
Every day brought me closer to a culture barely infected by the outside world. In 1948, this experience was singular, unavailable in North America.

One of the reasons for this was the isolation in which the Hopi villages were fortunate enough to have been kept — an isolation from the rest of the world guarded by the thousands of square miles of desert surrounding them, the total lack of roads, and a desire to remain so isolated. The Hopis knew in their wisdom that the approaches of the whites would eventually destroy their way of life, their sacred path, the Hopi Way unless it could be stopped.

The Hopi way of life, I learned from observation through Leslie, whom I learned to love like a brother, was unlike any other in its protectiveness of custom.

As the first rays of the sun, the father, pierced through the early morning mist, filtering through the grey legions of the Arizona sky, the tiny opening of my roof top abode was ablaze. Stiffened by a night on a sheepskin — the only bed I had — the first thing taught to me is that a Hopi man greets *Father Sun* with a blessing of sacred corn meal.

Feeling the dampness of the white clay with which Hopi roofs are made, I would take a pinch of corn meal from the little bag Leslie had given me as my own and, facing the rising sun, I would say a prayer "inside of me" (as the Hopis put it) something like:

> *Oh my father without whom*
> *nothing would grow.*
> *Bless this coming day,*
> *make me have a good life,*
> *and make me be better today*
> *than I have been yesterday.*

After *blowing* my prayer on the corn meal with my breath, I *sent* it to the Sun Father, lifting the corn meal toward its direction, letting it sprinkle the earth. A day started in that manner, the Hopis believe, will always be a good day.

Below me in the house, I could hear Leslie, Alta and some of the children busy with the folding of their own pallets, some inside, some on the roof tops. Perhaps the reader thinks that I would then go down the ladder to the house and, among the greetings of the whole family, exchange amenities before sitting at the table to have coffee. None of that accompanied the start of a new day at Hopi in those days. Instead, I would come down from my tiny rooftop room, leaving the black eagle tied to the

34

roof. In the main part of the house I was greeted by total silence.

None of the Caucasian amenities like "Good morning" — who knows yet how good it is? — "Did you sleep well?" — if you did not, it makes only for idle conversation — or, "How are you, today?" — never an honest question in our society, or an honestly answered one.

The Hopis' total sense of accuracy would not allow these half-truths, or complete untruths, to start a day in such an unholy

Leslie on "Charley" going to the spring for water.

manner. So it is begun in silence. Living among the Hopis at the end of the forties (fifty years after famous photographers Edward Curtis and A.C. Vroman stayed with them) taught me the great virtue of silence. a beautiful substitute for rambling nonsense.

Clinging to my Caucasian ways, though, I would dip into the steel container in which they kept rain, spring water, or a combination of the two in order to wash my face and teeth, a *luxury* everyone tolerated because I was the "Bahana," white person (also written Pahana), of the household, but no one else would do it, water being precious as gold on top of a Hopi mesa. Later on, Leslie and I saddled his donkey, Charley, and went to a distant spring with two ten-gallon tin containers that hung from Charley's flanks. You had to be a part of the ritual to understand the price of a single dip of drinking water. The trails resembled stairways to the upper floors of a Manhattan skyscraper.

One thing I always say about Hopi life: it was not dull. Between getting water at the water holes, or springs, depending on the time of the year; digging for coal in the family mine way deep in a canyon when cold weather set in; working in the fields; trading for meat with the Navajos; preparing or participating in the Catcinup (kachina) Ceremonials, Powamu, Soyal or Wuwuchim, you would appreciate that Hopi life was indeed very interesting, with no time left over for any unproductive thinking.

But going back to the morning: Alta would spread a blanket on the floor and set a large Hopi bowl in the center of it, cups, a pot of fresh coffee, Hopi bread and, without further delay, after Leslie formulated a Hopi blessing, everyone dipped their fingers in the mutton and hominy stew.

Among so many fond memories of my Hopi life, perhaps this single event, repeated every morning, seated crosslegged or on my knees, dipping three fingers and a piece of fry bread to catch hominy and mutton, heading it for my mouth without losing it in the process, stands out as the warmest welcome of the new day. Indeed, there is something unique and mysterious in the coming of an early morning on a high mesa in the great desert of northern Arizona.

Still surrounded by the golden silence that the Hopis observe as a way of life, Leslie would stand up when finished and sit on his favorite small bench near the window. I knew he was thinking about what our first activity for the day would be. Whatever it was, I would silently go up the ladder to my highrise residence to put on my moccasins, shirt and cowboy hat so I would be protected from the sun and the harshness of the Hopi trails.

I would give a friendly glance to the magnificent black eagle standing next to me chained to a log, his bright yellow beak and talons contrasting with the black lustrous shine of his feathers.

Each clan member at Hopi had the right to catch a young eagle in the spring in the cliffs surrounding the mesas, sometimes forty or fifty miles away. Each Hopi clan had ancestral eagle nests reserved for the members of a particular clan. Because of the sacredness of the magnificent bird, it would bless a household by its very presence, becoming, in actuality, a member of the family until the village Niman Catcina Ceremony — the going home ceremony in late July when the Catcinas are thought to leave the Hopi villages to retire in the San Francisco peaks above Flagstaff until the following November when they return for the first ceremony of the new Catcina year, the new-fire ceremony.

— It is then ceremonially sacrificed after being blessed and loaded with messages to take to the spirit world. Its feathers are kept and used in the ceremonies. So he remains with his Hopi brothers forever. The body is placed in a cemetery for eagles as if it were human.

My writing, it should be known, is not the scientific report of an anthropological researcher. There have been plenty of those. It is, rather, a telling of what I went through at the hands of a very small social group who taught me the uniqueness of life; that man is the equal, not the superior, of animal, vegetable, mineral and cosmic worlds.

This, of course, was in complete contradiction to what I had been raised to believe. In order to accept such a teaching, I had to step down in my anthropomorphic thoughts, just as I descended the ladder from my room every morning.

Sleeping in the tiny room, four and a half feet wide, six feet long on top of Alta's and Leslie's house, a room used as a storage place for skins, dried peaches and baskets, taught me simplicity and humility. My belongings were a backpack, a sheepskin, a pillow...no more than the possessions of a Tibetan monk.

The bird's-eye view I had from my room to the sky, the eagle, the smell of this alcove built hundreds of years before, contributed in transporting me backward in time—to the days when the Hopis were free, protected by the desert, the cliffs, their indomitable beliefs.

At times, I also slept with the whole family, either on top of another larger house or, in bad weather, on the floor of the living /dining/sleeping room.

Of all the elements leading to my own metamorphosis, it was

the silence imposed by so few people living in such an immense space that, I recall, was the most powerful.

In contemporary American life there is rarely, if ever, a place where someone can experience the formidable volume of silence. At Hopi, it was and is everywhere all the time, forcing you to look *inside* for solace instead of outside.

Hopi people, although friendly, use words only if filled with meaning. If we were to take the words without meanings out of our modern everyday life, perhaps silence would again appear comforting.

Another peaceful element of transformation for me was the sweet prevalent smell of corn. Corn, the staff of life for the Hopis, stored in huge bins in the houses. Ground, cooked, eaten at each meal, sprinkled as holy cornmeal everywhere. At Hopi you are drowning in the sweet smell of corn as it permeates every place you go in the village.

What was happening with all of this was so fundamental that the very essence of my being was caught in a vise that squeezed the non-essential out of me leaving the real me, finally extrapolated from all the excess baggage left by thirty years of pressures, ineffective teachings and false concepts. As a result, I sometimes found myself in a vacuum, the old moving out, the new not yet there.

My Hopi friends could see this and, in their wisdom, said nothing. It had to happen, they knew that. I was a new babe, or rather, a reborn one, surrounded by the essentials of life. It made me think of the withdrawals I so often read about in addictions; my withdrawal was psychological. From a Frenchman raised in the sophistication of Parisian life, I was emerging into a world of Hopi values. Everything I was getting now was from Mother Earth.

The Hopis, in the majesty of their humble lives, were going at the business of life, knowing I was there and not ignoring it but not interfering either. They did not ask questions or hint at the pressures I felt. Loving, for them, was accepting; I had plenty of that, enough to sustain me.

I was being given the ultimate lesson of my life, one I could never forget. I had been a long time looking for it and now I was getting to the end of the tunnel I had entered when I was born.

The day I entered Hopi life, not only did I find myself part Hopi culturally speaking, but also religiously, I might add. The main current of spiritual and religious life at Hopi is the Catcina or Catcinup cult which supersedes everything from eating to walking in the fields, making love or anything else. I fell deeply in love with this concept of life.

My Christian upbringing had left a lot of unanswered questions, ever since catechism. My feeling for the Catcinas, my understanding of them, filled all the holes.

I would not quit loving the Lord and the things He taught us, but a lot of the Judeo-Christian interpretations of His teachings made no sense to me, never had. In contrast, the Hopi Catcina ceremonies explained it all. Obviously, that form of understanding of both cosmos and planet Earth was something I could use and use it I did on a daily basis. It was like the water from the sky which we dipped and drank, and also worked for — sustaining, nourishing, necessary, omnipresent only when you looked for it.

Catcinas, as impersonated by members of the Catcina Society in the Hopi villages, are essentially the actualization of the spirit of things they represent which are everywhere. For instance, there is a Sun Catcina, Eagle Catcina, Morning Star Catcina, Antelope Catcina, et cetera, perhaps two hundred or more different ones, representing a whole universal pantheon.

Catcinas are considered teachers also. Through dances, rituals, song and ceremonies, they teach children and adults the intricacies of what it is to be a creature of the Great Spirit.

These unearthly beings of incomparable strength and beauty gave my life sounds and impressions that cannot be erased. It takes only once to hear the rhythm of their dancing feet on the roofs of the kivas as they descend through the ladders into them with the powerful melodies of the Catcina songs, to imprint on the memory a lifetime meaning.

Wuwuchim, Soyal and *Powamu* are the main yearly cycles of the Catcina ceremonies. Through them, I learned how it feels to be a Hopi as I had the latent need to grasp the sacred in things since childhood. *Feeling* is the Indian way of grasping as opposed to the Germano-Greco-Latin interpretation of understanding through reasoning. Feeling is real while reasoning is a mechanical discipline, a mental attitude which makes the world fit into any necessary dogma.

My inner transformation was growing stronger every day, preparing me for more to come.

Leslie and the family seemed to have no doubts about me growing into a fuller Hopi dimension. In fact, an incredible event was about to take place, most incredible for me, but most of all for the Hopis of Shipaulovi who seemed to have understood it even better than I did.

I had had a very hard day in the fields one day before, Hopi fields being miles from the village. Because Leslie was busy doing something else, I went to rest on top of a small rocky mesa opposite the village. It was there that, sprawled on the flat warm rock, I fell into a deep hypnotic sleep. The midday sun was bathing my body with intense rays. In this translucid state of mind, I saw a tall human-like being appear before me. His long blond wavy hair fell below his shoulders.

"My name is Somiviki," he said, "I have come to tell you that you will have your own clan. It will be called the Banana Clan."

When I awoke from this unexpected dream, there was no way I could keep it to myself. I had to confide in Leslie. I knew the experience was real, not merely a dream.

When Alta called me for lunch across the rocky abyss which separated the village from Soyok Mesa on which it happened, I ran the distance in a few short minutes.

"Leslie..." I began impatiently as everyone silently dipped their fingers in the bowl of rabbit stew.

A long silence followed, I imagined my relationship with my Hopi family ruined by the audacity of my mouth. A sacrilege, I thought.

Then Leslie and his whole family burst into a loud, unrestrained laugh.

"Banana Clan!!!" exclaimed Leslie, grinning widely, choking with laughter.

They knew, each of them, that banana was my improper

hearing of the Hopi word for white man. Bahana. My vision had been real, but not without humor. In the years that followed, the friends I brought to Hopi were always classified as "bananas," clear to this day. The little children of the village running around chanting: "Banana Clan...Banana Clan..." sweet music to my ears, like running water.

The Banana Clan prospered away from Hopi as if I had taken a slice of Hopi ceremonial life with me.

Leslie knew all of this much before I did. His ability to perceive things that have no logical explanation was indeed uncanny.

We were in one of his corn and squash fields one day, far from the village. The drought had been severe that year. "I don't know how I'll be able to bring green corn to the Niman Catcinup," he said to me. "My corn is so small...we need rain." He looked sad when he said that.

The Niman is the last masked sacred dance of the Catcina year held in late July, the one after which the Catcinas go back to their spiritual home in the San Francisco peaks above Flagstaff, awaiting the following opening of the sacred season in December.

"Why don't you shoot an arrow straight at the sun," he said to me. "Then we'll have rain."

I always carried a sixty-pound aluminum steel bow with me in the fields to shoot rabbits. Without thinking, I sent an arrow to the sun. Now more than three or four minutes elapsed before a cloud darkened over Leslie's field where we were standing; the arrow never came down, but the rain did.

I recall another incident in which my handling of the bow added to the semi-mythical view the Hopis of Shipaulovi and Mishongnovi had of me.

Below the mesa upon which these two villages are built, perhaps three or four hundred feet below, the government built a school at a place called Toreva. Next to it they had built a laundry and a few showers for the Hopis.

One day, having offered a ride to a few ladies from the

41

village to go wash, I was waiting and practicing shooting arrows in the hill behind the laundry. Accuracy in shooting depends on constant practice.

Of course, as always, several young boys accompanied me and were very interested in this "Bahana" who could shoot a can at seventy-five to a hundred feet. One of them said to me, "You cannot shoot on top of the mesa."

Without a word I cocked an arrow on the string of my bow and, shooting almost vertically above my head and in the direction of the village, I let the arrow fly.

To this day I cannot explain it. The arrow came down exactly in the front door of my friend Leslie's house on top of the mesa. To get there the arrow had to have travelled a mile.

Writing this, I shiver at the thought it could have hurt someone — or worse. However, living in the dimension I lived in then, nothing negative could have happened, only good.

Naturally all of these incidents brought me farther into the intricate fabric of Hopi life so when the time for a ritual rabbit hunt came, as part of a little boy's initiation, I was asked to participate.

Early in the morning of the *Coushimamaka*, as the whole rabbit hunt ceremony is called, the young boy going through the initiation ceremony — he was around twelve — was dressed in ceremonial clothes. That is, he was wearing the *pitchcuna* — the embroidered kilt Hopis wear for their ceremony — his body painted with red and black stripes, tufts of eagle feathers in his hair, a couple of painted ceremonial throwing sticks — resembling very much the Australian boomerang but somewhat larger — in his hands. As the sun rose, the family of the boy gave a feast of ceremonial food: stew, pies and *pikami* — pudding cooked in an earth pit. Most of the villagers came to eat.

Around nine or ten o'clock in the morning the men of the village gathered on the desert floor at the foot of the mesa. Perhaps thirty men were there that day. They were mostly silent, exchanging brief comments on where they would start the hunt.

Soon after, three or four young unmarried girls wearing black mantas and white and red ceremonial shawls, their faces

Morning of COUSHIMAMAKA. Little boy dressed in ceremonial clothes.

painted white and harboring the traditional butterfly hairdo of
Hopi maidens, joined the party.

Some on foot, some on donkeys or horses, the crowd headed
for the desert of sage and brush four or five miles from the mesa
and started forming a huge circle a quarter of a mile in diameter.

At a signal, the men started walking toward the center of this
huge circle, yelling and beating the bushes with their throwing
sticks. As the circle got smaller and smaller, the rabbits got thicker
and thicker.

When a rabbit was hit, one of the ceremonial maidens would
run to get it and bring it back to a man who carried a gunny sack
for her; in exchange, she gave the hunter a handful of somivikis, a
Hopi ceremonial delicacy resembling a Mexican tamale but with
blue corn meal mush inside. I suspect that the Mexican delicacy is
a derivative of the somiviki which the Spanish people adopted as
they cohabited in Indian country.

Back to the mesa top in the evening, all the ladies were busy
preparing the rabbits — perhaps sixty or seventy that day — to
be roasted in outdoor ovens sealed with stone plaques and mud.
Dehydrated and cooked, rabbit meat can be preserved for a

43

Leslie hunting rabbit.

whole year. Dehydration as a method for preserving food was used by the Hopis from time immemorial.

*   *   *

Living with the Hopi people taught me that dimensions could be brought about by dreaming, praying, desiring, though the latter is not to be confused with anything prurient or selfish. The desire, as it were, must be free of personal gratification for the good of all. Thus, living with these gentle desert dwellers did not bring limitations to the forms in which one operates. What would have been impossible to men and women living under limited potential becomes thoroughly possible in the Hopi context of everyday living. There were no miracles, only realities.

What follows is also typical of life at Hopi in the forties during a time when white encroachment had not yet made them self-conscious of what subsequently became falsely called "childlike" feelings.

When I came to live at Hopi, crime, even petty crime, was

44

unknown. There was no name for it in the Hopi language.

Alta had six children from her previous marriage, one elder son and five girls. Of course, Leslie was raising the girls left at home, together with the three boys they had together.

Patsy was twelve or thirteen at the time of this story. Hopis did not register their children, so it was always difficult to know exactly how old someone was. She had lost one eye to a disease, which often occurred among desert tribes due to the harsh conditions in which they lived. She also was born with a deformed left hip probably due to malnutrition and she walked with a limp.

I usually used the noon meal when everyone was present to launch one of my requests. Hopis consult each other on all serious matters and this was an acceptable time.

Everyone was attentive.

"I am getting ready to go to California for a trip," I said, "and I would like to take Patsy with me. She needs to see a doctor to save her good eye."

Complete silence followed. Then Leslie and Alta carried on a conversation in Hopi while they were eating. It was ten minutes before Leslie appeared ready to say something to me.

"From now on," he said, "you will be Patsy's father. She will be your daughter."

Leslie's decision to go along with my request had completely reoriented their family unit. My question would have been, at the very least, completely ordinary in the white society. Here it required changing the entire structure of a family relationship. I had never thought of that. Leslie did what he had to do. An act of adoption had been completed within minutes. Hopi life and order was again intact, and I had acquired a daughter with whom I would leave for California in two days.

Until her death, which happened a few years ago, she called me Dad and requested my assistance many times as her father. Patsy now lies in one of the sand dunes the Hopis use as their burial grounds, part of the land they love so much, only a short distance from the village which nurtures and strengthens them to remain what they are.

45

I needed no more assurance that the family considered me a full-fledged member. Nevertheless, something else happened one day and that alone, if nothing else, would have given me the total satisfaction of knowing that, in their minds, I was part of the structural edifice of a Hopi family.

It happened as I was coming back from California and the truck which had given me a lift from Winslow deposited me, with my old army backpack on my back, at the foot of Second Mesa.

I knew the trail which climbs through the steep vertical cliff well. It took me twenty minutes, perhaps to get to the first ledge of the mesa on which Mishongnovi is built. In fact, I was next to where my good friend Wesley had his house. To take a breather, I went in to see if he was home. The whole family was having supper on the floor, as usual, a huge pot of stew in the midst of everyone.

"Come and eat," Wesley said. That is a formal greeting that no one is allowed to refuse at Hopi. So I sat and ate with them.

Wesley was a wonderful storyteller, well-known among his people. After dinner he talked for a long while. Night had come, it was raining.

"Stay with us till morning," Wesley said. "By then the trail will be dry and you can go home to Shipaulovi."

The suggestion seemed reasonable and as an extra mattress was brought for me amidst the dozens of others, I slept soundly all night, the livingroom transformed for the night into a family dormitory.

When I prepared to leave Wesley in the early morning to climb to Shipaulovi, I was apprehensive, without knowing exactly why. The climb was a short one, through a short cut with boulders that stand above the kivas in the west side of the village. Opening the door of the house, I saw Alta working at her eternal plaque. As mentioned earlier, a plaque is a basket which is flat and looks like a plate. It is made by Hopi ladies of Second Mesa only (Shipaulovi, Mishongnovi, Shumopovi), along with other types of baskets, it is constructed with coils of grass surrounded by split yucca leaves and decorated with colorful designs of flowers, Catcina masks or animals.

Alta did not lift her head from her work, saying nothing to greet me. At once I knew something was wrong. I deposited my bag in a corner of the room and, sitting on Leslie's small bench, I asked where he was.

"He left for his fields early this morning," she said, "and he did not even take anything to eat!"

Now I knew something was terribly wrong, and I was the cause of it.

"I baked a pie for you last night but you did not come home to eat it." Hopis don't need formal practical knowledge that someone is coming; they know it through long practice of psychic intelligence.

"It is the custom that you go to your home first and greet your family, then you can go to visit your friends. This is your home, we are your family. This is why your brother went to his fields, saddened."

Paul Coze had taught me a lot of Hopi "dos and don'ts," but none to cover this. Nor had my experiences with them prepared me for such a grandiose mistake — the only serious mistake I ever made, but it taught me one thing: I had become a Hopi as a member of Leslie's family and I never forgot it after that.

Another year passed before drastic changes entered my life and by then my marriage had completely collapsed. I suppose I could have saved it if I had not gone to live with the Hopis, but my move was irrevocable and my attraction to the desert and its inestimable silence irresistable. Trying to explain it to myself, I had to resort to reincarnation. It was the only explanation which made any sense. If I had been Indian in another lifetime, my longing for their ways might seem less self-conscious and directed by willpower.

Incidentally, I remember a time when Leslie, Alta and I made an excursion into Navajo country to trade Hopi peaches (apricots) for mutton, badly needed for our meals. After storing several crates of these small peaches which the early Spanish friars had brought to the Hopis long ago, in the back of a horsedrawn wagon, we went on an expedition for two and a half days!

The way the Hopis and Navajos traded with each other can

47

only be fully understood by someone living with them. The trade was based on the concepts upon which their lives were rooted: respect of each other beyond the distrust which had existed between them since historic times.

First, we would approach a hogan no closer than several hundred feet. There was a long wait in total immobility and silence. Perhaps fifteen minutes later or more, the rug which served as a door for the Navajo hogan moved slightly, indicating somebody watching us. Another ten minutes or so later, a Navajo woman slowly, very slowly approached our wagon, head slightly lowered toward the ground. Her walk was silent in moccasined feet and only the swishing of a pleated silk skirt revealed her presence. The unusual hair style, velvet blouse with silver buttons, a striking portrait, Navajo women were part of the desert itself, spring flowers dotting the landscape.

After looking in the bushel baskets full of apricots, still without a word, the woman went back to the hogan. Ten minutes passed, she reappeared, holding dry mutton, wrapped loosely in newspapers. After handing it to Alta, not to Leslie, she waited at the back of the wagon until Alta handed her a bushel of the small yellow fruits which the Navajos were so fond of.

Alta would add a small canful to show the trade was complete, no cheating had taken place, everybody was happy, freeing us to go to another hogan and repeat the trade.

*   *   *

A true account of my life at Hopi would not be complete without saying that although the people were conditioned by centuries of acclimatization to harsh desert conditions, once in a while deprivations, climate or bad crops would lead to some severe setbacks.

It was such a condition I found years later in the spring of 1968 when, after staying away from Hopi for more than a year and a half, I found the people of Shipaulovi in a badly rundown state. An epidemic of measles had hit about every child in the village. The trend, at the time, was to stay away from the government hospital in Keams Canyon, the Hopis mistrusting white medicine.

The winter had been very severe and the crops of the preceding summer scarce. Very few men had been able to work for cash, so there wasn't any around.

Even warm clothing and blankets were few in this cold snap of early spring. I thought the situation so critical, in fact, that I didn't stay but three or four days, having in mind to do something about it on my own. I had already settled in Santa Fe by then, and upon my return, I organized a drive through which I collected more than a ton of food, vestments, blankets, and so forth. The generosity of friends, relatives, even strangers was incredible. They could see my concern and the dire need.

In the process, a close friend, a retired army colonel, proceeded to help me with the drive. A local businessman, Dick Hughes, being in the automotive business and also showing concern with my preoccupations, loaned me a two-ton truck filled with gas. One late afternoon after work, the colonel and I set out for Hopi at the wheel of the truck, filled to the brim. I brought a used Frigidaire, now that the Hopis had electricity hooked up by the government the year before. I thought the children, this way, would be able to have milk. It was the first ice box brought to the village.

We arrived at daybreak, finding everyone in the relative warmth of their beddings. It is impossible, really, to describe accurately the reception we received: a mixture of Santa Claus and a common, everyday miracle.

The whole morning was spent making allotments to each family in the village, amidst laughing, crying and joyful faces of every Hopi. I felt extremely privileged to have been able to live in this moment of gratitude — my own — for, after all they had done to liberate me, I was finally able to return the warm blanket of friendship to them.

In the summer of 1954, the need to spend some time with my Hopi family became urgent.

Although still very shaky, my marriage and, therefore, my life in San Francisco with my two children, was still a reality. I had "bitten the bullet" and was making money as a factory representative for several cosmetic concerns. My main line was "Prince Matchabelli" and I employed agents in a large territory from San Luis Obispo to Eureka.

Having others on the job representing my line enabled me to take leaves of absence pretty much as I saw fit. This time I asked my wife if she would let me have my daughter on the trip to Hopi country. I was apprehensive about her answer.

"You can have *your* daughter for the trip as long as *my son* stays with me."

I was surprised but happy. France (I gave my daughter that name since she was born right after the military collapse of my former country) was to be not only a delightful companion although only ten at the time, but also the Hopi world would change her life as it had mine.

She blended right in with the Hopi children, and it was only a couple of weeks after we arrived that the "name-giving ceremony" for young girls was to be performed and Alta decided she should be part if it.

In the traditional black manta, white boots and butterfly hair style that unmarried Hopi girls wear, my little girl looked amazingly Hopi. I couldn't believe it. She was then given the name "Tawamana," Sun Girl, in a ceremony which touched on initiation but is for the purpose of getting a new name different from the one girl children receive at birth. In the first name-giving ceremony, the child is kept twenty days without exposure to sunlight, after which she is presented to the Sun Father at sunrise of the twentieth day,

A ceremonial feast followed the ceremony. Alta gave her the new name which, of course, has to do with the adoptive mother's clan which gives the name. Alta's clan was the Sun Clan and therefore she named France the Sun Girl.

We spent some very happy moments at Hopi, some of my happiest, in fact. Seeing my own daughter partake of a way of life I had already adopted was of great consequence.

During my numerous stays at Hopi, my most difficult moments were always when I prepared to leave to go back to work and live with my blood family.

However, this time it was easier: France was with me and I decided not to go back right away, but to extend our trip to Taos, New Mexico where my old friend, Worthington Hagerman, the American Consul who was in Lisbon during my stay there and who was responsible for my coming to America, had retired to paint in this artists' mecca.

According to custom no goodbyes were given when we left for New Mexico. Hopis — and Indians in general — do not like to say goodbye as they believe that leaving is the first step toward coming back.

As my little girl and I were driving toward Taos, reflecting on all my Hopi experiences, a certain sadness permeated my whole being. Certainly I would go back. I knew that I could never be separated from my Hopi family for very long, but somehow, I knew also that my life was in transition because the more I had learned about the Hopi Way, the more I realized that its innermost purpose was to prepare me for another step.

Understanding the divine balance between body, mind and spirit which the Hopis harmonized into the universal flow — so

My daughter France at name giving ceremony. Next to her is Frieda.

My Hopi family: Leslie with black bandana, Alta to his right, Patsy next to the door. My room on top of the roof.

that all actions might pass swiftly from one stage to another, on this plane or another — was everything I knew up to that point. But this also taught me that since everything is to a greater purpose, the next step to any further personal evolution must necessarily be unknown — at least for a time.

3 TAOS

.After arriving in Taos, we stayed at my friend's house. His young French wife, Marcelle, was a wonderful hostess, attending to our every wish and making our stay delightful.

The next day after our arrival, I decided to go to the Indian pueblo for a visit. When in Flagstaff, Paul had introduced me to the pueblo Lieutenant Governor and I wanted to see him again.

It was a coincidence, I thought, when I saw him at the pueblo entrance checking the flow of tourists.

"Cruz!"

"Hello, Robert."

Cruz Trujillo was a big man, handsome and friendly. "Come," he said, "I want to take you around. Why don't you let your little girl play with that girl over there." He was pointing toward a slender twelve or thirteen-year-old Indian girl, tall for her age, with beautiful dark skin.

Addressing himself to France, he said, "Her name is Mary Janice. She will play with you while I show the pueblo to your dad."

Taos Pueblo sits at the base of high rugged mountains, the waters of a mountain stream dividing two adobe "apartment" complexes into Winter and Summer Clans; these are fronted by a plaza or courtyard as big as a military exercise field. Nearby, there is a mission church several centuries old.

It was not before mid-afternoon and many stops at people's houses for coffee and Indian bread that I asked, "Where do you think my little girl is, Cruz?"

"Don't worry," he said. "She's at her friend's mother's place. We'll stop to pick her up after I show you our church."

On the way I thought how magnificent the Pueblo of Taos was and, somehow thinking back through the centuries, what a vision it must have been for the Spanish Conquistadors finding this pearl of a community, cuddled among the mountains after travelling thousands of miles through harsh desert terrain.

Of all the pueblos and Indian villages of Arizona and New Mexico, I would put Taos next in magnificence to the charismatic feelings given the traveler by the high mesas of the Hopis.

The Pueblo of Taos is actually composed of two pueblos.

The Northern Compound, which is six stories high, and the Southern which varies from two to three. They are separated by a torrent of a river coming down from sacred Blue Lake at the 12,000 foot level. The river is the only source of Pueblo drinking water.

I often imagine the thrill those armored horsemen certainly had when they first saw the glittering walls of the pueblo in the light of the setting sun. No wonder they thought it was made of gold. (It was, but of a gold that cannot be melted down and which lasts forever.)

The pueblo they saw and we see today is not the only one that existed. A short distance toward the north, the ruins of a more ancient pueblo on a higher elevation are well guarded and forbidden soil to the outsider. Destroyed perhaps one or two centuries before the arrival of the Spaniards, no one seems to know exactly what the circumstances of its destruction were — warfare, epidemic, fire — whatever the circumstances, the people moved a little way down river and built another pueblo.

Taos also had several sister pueblos speaking the same tongue, Tiwa. Buried some distance to the east, they appear to have been very large indeed, similar to the one at Pot Creek which I just mentioned. Picuris is still standing, active and prospering, speaking the same language as the Taosenos.

One remarkable thing about Taos is the size of what could be called its "plaza." It seems more like a military exercise field by the size of it. The remnants of a defense-wall surrounding the pueblo are still visible, although perhaps half as tall as they once were Every year, Cruz told me, the population of the pueblo is committed to mud-plaster the entire village and they also plaster the enclosing wall several miles long, a sacred commitment to a glorious past.

Taos Pueblo is recognized as one of the great architectural marvels. Every year people from all over the world come to visit it, at times to the dismay of its inhabitants. Privacy is greatly threatened when thousands of tourists and sightseers walk up and down the Pueblo's streets and alleys. Photographs, paintings, renderings of the pueblo can be found the world over and justly so, for the place conjures an aura of antiquity and spiritual strength that cannot be imagined elsewhere.

During the long conversation with Lieutenant Governor Cruz that day, I learned that the people are somewhat different than in the other pueblos of the Southwest. Because of its northern location, Taos, in historical times, was a trading center, the link between other Indian groups living in the Rockies or the Great Plains, in what is now Kansas, Idaho and Texas.

These southern tribes: Cheyennes, Kiowas, Comanches, Utes and many others, would come usually twice a year, in the spring and in the fall, to trade skins and dry meat for baskets, pottery, jewelry and the like.

During these expeditions, warfare was suspended. A lot of merry-making would go on and, of course, courtships and marriages would follow, accounting for the fact Taosenos have — not only historically but genetically as well — traits that can be traced to the warriors of the Plains.

Ceremonies were borrowed from the Plains cultures, dances and rituals were exchanged, accounting for a Taos Pueblo culture somewhat different from the rest of the Rio Grande pueblos.

Like all Indian pueblos of New Mexico, Taos is officially Catholic, because it had been a condition for their sovereignty when conquered by the invading Spaniards in the 14th century. But I knew, as Paul Coze told me many times, that their own indigenous religion was always very strong, as the kivas from which the tall ladders point toward the sky testified.

Soon after visiting the little church, we dropped over to Mary Janice's house to pick up France. Cruz was right, she was playing with three girls and acting as if she had lived there all her life. And standing in the doorway of this small one-story house was the most beautiful Indian woman I had ever seen!

"Come in," she said. "My name is Mary. I am Mary Janice's mother." If she had said that she was the Queen of Sheba, I would not have been more amazed.

57

I was so impressed by the dignified appearance of that woman that I couldn't answer her greeting. However, silence is so much a part of the Indian world that it was okay not to speak and

I continued to stare at the lovely apparition before me.

Finally, I managed to say, "I am France's father."

She was wearing a spotless white fiesta dress, lavender shawl thrown over her shoulders. A beautiful smile, full of love and compassion, so typically and beautifully Indian. As far as I could tell, she might have been a descendant of Marina, the Indian

Mary in her ceremonial clothes.

woman who led Cortez to Tenochtitlan, capital of the Aztecs.

Mary was the synthesis and the archetype of all Indian races; she could have been Sioux, Cheyenne, Aztec or Inca, but her grace transcended all of them.

She had jet black hair caught in two large braids. Her eyes, of a deep brown color, gave the feeling of a warm alert nature. High cheek bones and the strong nose which distringuishes North American Indians from any other group, gave her an aristocratic air. Her mouth was full but indicated force of will and character.

Mary stood five feet seven or eight inches, which was unusual among Pueblos, but again, Taos had been at the crossroads between Pueblos and the warriors of the Plains. Here I could see a splendid example of the majesty and proud dignity of her people.

A wide Indian sash gripped a slender waist to complete what I could call a superb model for a willing painter. She was wearing those unique white boots that Taos Indian women wear and which add so much to their grace and appearance.

I wanted to feast my eyes on this splendid picture of a woman, but I knew I shouldn't forget that purest of Indian courtesies: not to stare. Giving glances only when I knew that she would not notice, I approached the doorway.

"Sir..."

"Robert," I said quickly, "please call me Robert."

"Well, Robert, would you have some watermelon with us?"

Her voice was firm, I could tell from hearing her speak that she was direct and honest but, at the same time, kind. She spoke with a melodious tone.

Cruz had to go back to his duties so this little feast of watermelon with Mary and her three girls was a delight for France and me and we took advantage of this magical time until we really had to go.

"Mary," I said, "I don't know how to thank you for your hospitality. France and I had such a great time."

"Please do come back to see us."

"We are only going to be in Taos for a couple of days or so."

"Why not come tomorrow and share lunch with us? My girls would love to play with France again."

She could not have said anything which pleased me more. I joyfully accepted. This visit had filled me with such indescribable pleasure that, back at my friend's house, I was on cloud nine as if the sun had burned away all the fog of my past life.

Lunch at Mary's house the next day was further proof of this mystical union. I held on to every moment believing that my very existence depended upon it but at the same time I was haunted by the gloom of having to leave this enchanted place and return home. I had to attend the fall agents' meeting in my "perfume territory."

In order to see Mary once more before we left, France and I dropped by her house to say goodbye. A terrible sadness filled my mind as we saw the adobe house for the last time.

Courteous and mannered as ever, Mary thanked us for having visited her and her family. She seemed calm and composed and I felt shaken and strange.

I managed to ask if I could take a picture of her before I left. So, leaning against my yellow and black Nash, my new-found Indian beauty made a memorable picture for me to remember her by. How could I imagine, then, that only minutes separated me from the shock of my life?

As I was backing the car out of her driveway, perhaps fifteen or twenty feet away from Mary — at the exact place where she would disappear from my sight — a beam, so bright I could not have been mistaken flashed from her eyes. Even with the distance separating us at that moment, I could not possibly have been wrong about it; it was a sign her mind was sending to me, a signal I had prayed for during the two days I had know her.

But now, I was gone...

For months after that, I could not forget that instant where, like a flash from heaven, Mary spoke to me without words.

Six months later, my business took me to another enchanted place, the big redwoods of the northwestern California coast. Every year at that time, I had to call on my trade in Eureka, California, the northern-most city in the state.

I liked that trip; from time to time I would stop the car under some redwood grove to walk under the majestic roof made by the kings of the forest, breathing in the smell of wet undergrowth, the moist dark earth of the forest.

Fifty miles south of Eureka I had two good friends, both sculptors, who owned about a hundred acres of redwoods. They had built two very comfortable cabins which were tucked away in the semi-darkness of the grove. One served as home and studio, the other as guest house.

I decided to stop since it was Saturday afternoon and my appointments were for Monday in Eureka. They were delighted to see me. Company was not an everyday occurrence in their neck of the woods.

The culinary skills of the two sculptors were equal to their art. After a wonderful evening meal, they insisted I bed down in the guest house.

A colossal stone fireplace occupied most of the cabin, a fireplace in which a small tree could have easily burned. Above it, there was a loft with a large comfortable bed topped by a thick down comforter such as I had not seen since my European days.

As I prepared myself for the night in solitude and silence, all sounds muffled by the huge trees towering above us, I thought of Mary far away in her little Indian pueblo in New Mexico. I thought of her often. The thought of writing to her was constantly on my mind. But I dismissed it as foolish. Now, as the flames brightened the room and the redwood logs crackled, I thought of it again. Why not?

I had to find out if she remembered me, if what I saw in her eyes was my own wish actualized in my own mind or, perhaps, something else.

I spent a good portion of the night writing. All my frustrated constricted wishful thinking spilled upon page after page. When I was through, I wondered if I would ever have the courage to send it to her. What if she felt insulted by my romantic style. After all, her culture was so different in those matters than the Frenchman who lets his feelings run wild in a solitary night under the redwood trees.

I sent it, though, the next day in Eureka, bringing unto myself the nightmare of going to the San Francisco main post office each time I wanted to check and see if she would answer. I had given her a general delivery address, in case she might feel inclined.

For weeks and weeks I waited in vain. My hopes of getting an answer were about gone when I said to myself, "I'll go once more."

The clerk had looked many times in the pile of General Delivery letters when I called on him, so that I was totally unprepared when he handed me a small, square envelope. I think I was shaking, I could hardly reach the wooden bench closest to me; my legs wobbled uncertainly.

Nevertheless, here it was, an answer to my letter. Thoughts came rushing to my mind. Is this a polite answer to my emotional explosion? Is she telling me to stop writing?

It was well written but short.

As far as I was concerned it needn't have said more than this one sentence: "I felt exactly the way you did when you left my home."

I couldn't believe it; all those months I had not been wrong; we both felt deeply toward each other. I would have liked to write on the spot, call, send a telegram, let her know the ecstasy her letter had brought to me.

However, the Indian telegram, a psychic message, was best; I sent her my gratitude, my devotion, my strongest desire.

It was this way Red River Flower and I fell deeply in love!

Letters followed letters, and over the months, we began to know each other. We wrote of our lives, our wishes. We made plans. But letters, no matter how beautiful (and Mary's were, in their simplicity and directness) are only beginnings. I longed to see her again.

Hopi had brought me the first understanding of the Indian soul. Mary was now showing me the whole truth of her being, her way of thinking, her Indian-ness.

I was discovering that not only had a woman entered my life, but an entire people, the totality of the Indian soul, perhaps, an archetype of the feminine psyche as well. Growing impatient to see each other, we started to plan an elopement for the coming fall. She would find a babysitter for her children, we would spend a few days together.

Mary had been married previously to a Zuni man. She had been divorced from him for several years when I met her. She had four children from that union.

The plan was to pick her up in front of the La Fonda de Taos on a specified day. I was very excited as plans grew more definite but not without certain misgivings. After all, her life was totally Indian, her pueblo was two thousand miles away. With her large family many things could go wrong.

As the dream came closer to reality with each passing day, I conceded to myself that dreams sometimes stay dreams.

One reality was that I had developed two small ulcers; I would have to nurse them. My body was reacting to the stress of my mind. But at the time I felt there was nothing I could do. Mary was in my thoughts constantly and so were my feats of failure.

Another problem was Mary's letters weren't so frequent and this added to my anxiety. Faith and faith alone sustained me during those last days when reason would have told me otherwise. I remembered how I felt when the days before meeting my Hopi friends became shorter and shorter: the disarray, the impatience, the worries, but it came to pass.

I arrived in Santa Fe after driving my stationwagon straight from San Francisco. I had driven all night and was exhausted. The first thing I wanted to do was to find the right place to take Mary after our meeting in Taos which was planned for the next day at four p.m.

Santa Fe in the mid-50s was not as big as it is now. In fact, I think the population was around 25,000. It was still a Southwestern frontier town, capital of a state that had joined the

Union only some forty-five years before, still very much Hispanic with all the charm of the northernmost capital of the Spanish dominions.

Hotels and motels were few, mostly concentrated downtown or at Santa Fe's southern entrance, Cerrillos Road, then a two-lane road as was the whole distance from Albuquerque.

The annual Santa Fe Fiesta with its many thousands of participants and visitors was about to happen. It was impossible to find a room downtown.

I thought that more lodging would be available on the northern side of town but I didn't know Santa Fe well and I was wrong. The only thing I found was a small sign saying: "San Juan Ranch 12 miles. Overnight accommodations."

On a hunch, I decided to try that. It proved to be the dustiest twelve miles of small winding road I had ridden over in a long time, sand hill after sand hill, covered by piñon trees. On the other side of the Tesuque Valley, I could see the tall green mountains of the Sangre de Cristo range.

The wilderness road ended finally and I entered the San Juan Ranch with its typical hacienda atmosphere of old time New Mexico. I would surprise some, I suppose, saying that what was the San Juan Ranch then is the Santa Fe Opera now. The four-lane highway had not yet been constructed and the only existing road north was through Tesuque.

The main house, with its lovely patio, large rooms and grand piano dominating the luxurious living room, was stately. Several small bungalows had been added — in the same Spanish style as the rest — to be rented to tourists and visitors.

It was very informal as I recall; no office and, walking into the living room, a tall thin man in his fifties was playing the piano. In the characteristically unbusinesslike fashion of those bygone times, he rented me the bungalow of my choice with a certain air that suggested he had much better things to do.

Nearby was a splendid swimming pool, reflecting the tall mountains in calm green water. I was so nervous during that first night that I stayed by the pool during most of it, nursing my reveries in this idyllic setting.

Many times life simplifies the things that our minds have made complicated for, the next day, it seemed so natural for me to take the road to Taos. I was supposed to meet Mary on the Plaza at four that day — if everything went well.

Taos, like Santa Fe, was then much smaller than it is now. Kit Carson's hometown resembled a small Spanish or, rather, Mexican villa of old. Practically all the businesses were assembled around its Plaza giving the appearance of a frontier fort, a tall flagpole in the center. Taos, because of Kit Carson's fame as a frontiersman and Indian fighter, had won the honor of keeping the colors waving day and night until the flag needed to be replaced. Or at least this is what I had been told.

Whirling around the Plaza looking for Mary, I came to a stop in front of La Fonda de Taos, the famous hotel where Lawrence-the-writer first exhibited the "lewd" paintings of Lawrence-the-artist.

There, dressed in a lovely blue fiesta dress, her beautiful eyes searching for mine, Mary stood before La Fonda with a little bag next to her beaded moccasins.

Jet black braids, bangs over the eyes framing her dark face, she gave me a renewed confidence that all was well.

We did not stay long in Taos. We wanted to be out of town as soon as possible, by ourselves. Stopping for a moment before going down the Canyon toward Pilar, the whole of the Rio Grande Gorge at our feet, we gave each other our first kiss.

It had been just a year since I met her at the pueblo. All these months of anxious waiting were back of us now. We were on our way to the San Juan Ranch where complete peace would be restored. However, amidst the exhilaration of this blissful time, a weird thing happened. We were happily talking, reunited at last when a wildly speeding car passed us, the driver either crazy, drunk, or both. At that time, just before the elementary school there was a bridge which went over a wide, dry arroyo. At ninety miles an hour, this car missed the bridge, hit the reinforced cement embankment and rolled over into the arroyo.

We stopped and found the man, thrown from his vehicle, lying in the sand, dead. We both prayed over him and then raced on to Española to report the event to the police. I have often thought about this morbid incident, wondering if it were a sign of some kind.

But whatever it was or might have been, our first evening together at San Juan Ranch was perfect.

The fact that this delightful spot became, in later years, the place where the Santa Fe Opera was built has always seemed significant to me. Now a divided highway links the Opera to nearby Santa Fe. No more twelve miles of romantic dirt road. But the old house and bungalows are.still here — a testimony (to me anyway) that Red River Flower and I spent unforgettable moments under the spell of the Sangre de Cristos.

We attended mass at the Santuario de Guadalupe next morning before eating breakfast in town and this offered me a glimpse of what Mary would graciously bring to my life.

I had not formally planned this trip in detail, but it turned out to have a conspicuous and delightful plan all its own — Carlsbad Caverns, El Paso, Juarez, coming back through Truth or Consequences, the hot springs. Way deep in the earth, perhaps a thousand feet into Carlsbad Caverns, there is a spot called the Queen's Chamber. Feeling both the mystery and the sacredness of the embrasure of Mother Earth, we deposited an eagle feather between two stalagmites which looked like an Indian shrine.

The little feather must still be there, a permanent testimony that we both offered it to Mother Earth as a silent prayer. The stillness and permanent silence of the boundless underworld place will probably keep our secret forever.

On our return trip to the pueblo seven days after leaving, we passed through Santa Cruz and Mary said to me, "My Aunt Isabel is the caretaker of a beautiful ranch here; why not stop and say hello?"

I agreed with enthusiasm.

"My Aunt Isabel raised me as a child," Mary added, "after my mother passed away. I consider her my mother. She is married to Uncle Pat Talachy, governor of the San Juan Pueblo."

Mary talked, my mind raced ahead of her. "Could we tell her of our plans?"

Our wedding day in front of Santa Fe's Cathedral.

She looked at me as she often did, deeply, as if looking inside me through the window of my eyes, a smile on her face.

"I could," she said. "I don't know how the idea of us getting married will strike her, you being from another race, but she loves me. Perhaps...stay in the car and pray; we may need it."

"That I will do," was my answer.

I knew it would be wonderful if Mary's family would agree to sponsor our marriage. The formal recognition of our union would make a very big difference in our future happiness, I knew; in fact a major difference, as Indians are bound by their families.

Mary had been gone for almost an hour when I saw her coming out through the huge carved door of the ranch's main house. She approached the car, a beautiful smile lighting her whole face. I knew then we had won.

I met Uncle Pat and Aunt Isabel that day and, learning they

would love us — each of us — like a mother and father, made me very confident.

Uncle Pat, in his great wisdom, would in fact teach me a great deal of the history of early Indian life in New Mexico. He was a scholar in his own right. He took me many times to the ruins of the old pueblo of San Gabriel, now called San Juan, which claims the honor of having been the first state capital when the invading Spaniards made it their headquarters in the 15th century.

Mary and I were married at the ranch, in a very intimate but very beautiful, ceremony the following first of January, Mary's birthday. Grandpa Concho, Uncle Pete and Aunt Easy, Uncle Pat and Aunt Isabel and perhaps a dozen more family members prepared a huge feast for us.

According to the matriarchal tradition of her people, we moved into a house on the Taos Pueblo which Aunt Isabel owned next to the village pasture. The place is called Phuanama, a very sacred place I was soon to discover.

"This house will be yours as long as you stay together," Aunt Isabel told us.

Six acres of land surrounded the house, six acres of cultivatable land that belonged to her and into which Mary and I and the children poured a lot of love and a lot of work. Mother Earth in her own infinite wisdom responded to that kind of attention a hundredfold and many a bushel of corn, beans or wheat testified to our belief and our work.

The house with its thirty-inch-thick adobe walls had a huge living area where Mary built a double bed supported by adobe walls, a kitchen, a store room and a good-sized family room for the children.

In front of the house, a small creek of crystal clear water was our water supply.

I didn't know it then, but I was going to be the first white man to live in the old way at the Pueblo of Taos. It had been a bold move, but as tradition required, I moved to my wife's home and the Taos people understood it that way, so we made many friends — friends who are still close after thirty years.

The author (center) with Juan Concho and son Robert.

At no time did the Taos people do anything to disturb our happiness; the family (numbering perhaps fifty people) accepted us from the start.

Only one man, a stubborn fellow named Safarino Martinez, twice governor of the pueblo, tried to run me out, without success. He was a mean character, part Mexican from way back. As governor, he wrote twice to the Indian Bureau in Washington, complaining of my presence. However, many elders in his own council were either from our family or friends of ours and he failed to do us any real harm.

I remember the time I caught him diverting water from the irrigation ditch going to our fields. It was at night because my fields were some of the last ones to use the ditch before the water left the reservation to be used by the Spanish Americans and Anglos of the township of Taos.

I had to change the water from one field to another and I woke up around midnight to do it. My eyes still heavy with sleep, I discerned what appeared to be a human form meddling in my corn field. I could not believe who it was: Safarino. I sprang upon him. Confused and silent, he left immediately with no fight. After that, he didn't even dare cross my path at the pueblo or even look straight at me!

Being on the road serving the cosmetic lines I still maintained and representing the factories that made them throughout four states, did not deter me from raising crops necessary for my family's survival, sometimes even selling them for cash.

I grew the tallest corn at the pueblo. I had pumpkins, all sorts of squashes, beans and a vegetable garden for our own use, plus goats, pigs and chickens.

I don't know how I found the energy to be on the road every other month and cultivate six acres of land but I did.

I think one basic ingredient of our happiness was my being in love with our life as it was, unchanged and unchanging, the Indian way as exemplified by Mary. My acceptance was the Indian's acceptance; we were one.

Living at Taos Pueblo as a member of a "closed" community, husband, father of five, taught me more, on a human level, than

The author and part of his family. His wife is at his right.

my stay at Hopi. But my involvements were quite different in each of those places.

In Taos, of course, my life was full of responsibility and I wanted to measure up to it. Looking back, I believe I did pretty well. Mary was a good teacher, the best, loving, kind and able to live comfortably in more than one world.

As a full member of the extended Indian family, I was required to participate in community work, as it was then called. This involved plastering the walls of the pueblo with that rich golden mud which once inspired the Spaniards to call the pueblos the Seven Cities of Cibola, thinking they were cities made of gold.

Other communal works were: fencing pastures, ditch cleaning, inspection of weapons, etc. I never entered a kiva, strictly reserved for the members of Taos Kiva's Societies. Any indiscretion of this sort would have been severely punished.

Sacred ceremonies at Taos Pueblo were exclusively reserved for Taos-born pueblo citizens who were ritually initiated; this was unlike Hopi where certain kiva ceremonies were open to Indians from other tribes, even non-Indians.

Never, in all the years I lived at the pueblo, did I step out of bounds. It was the least I could do to show my appreciation toward Indians who had warmly adopted my presence as one of their own.

Mary participated in all the ceremonial duties required of a member of the pueblo. I would not have expected her to do otherwise. Never did the exercise of these duties interfere with her life as wife or mother. Her great innate wisdom always told her what to do in order to keep everything in balance.

The only exception she made in the ritual calendar of her people was that during the entire length of our marriage she never took part in the annual pilgrimage to Blue Lake. She, perhaps, in her compassionate way, wanted to show me how seriously she was taking her status of married woman, the trip involving several days in the mountains for most of the able residents of the pueblo.

Blue Lake was a holy place for Taos Indians. They believed it to be the place of emergence from which their people long, long ago surfaced from the underworld, a belief common to all pueblos.

Once a year, in a great display of faith, the majority of the pueblo takes to the mountains for the pilgrimage to Blue Lake. The trek is so ceremonially exacting that all outsiders, Indians or whites, are barred from it. Armed guards are placed at strategic points around Blue Lake so that no one outside the pueblo can sneak by.

Mary felt that I should be given the opportunity to experience the aura of the lake revered by her people. To give me that very special chance, along with two other members of her family, we planned a trip to Blue Lake which would not conflict with the pueblo's annual pilgrimage.

It took two days on horseback to reach the sacred spot through spectacular mountain country at ten and eleven thousand feet in altitude. Through scarcely-travelled trails, we climbed high passes until we saw the blue jewel, a volcanic lake so blue it appeared dreamlike. Surrounded by high mountains, calm and serene, Blue Lake is indeed an exalted body of water. It inevitably leads one to the myth of life's emergence from worlds virtually lost to the memory of man.

Four little boys fished for us along the way, using their hands quick as the trout themselves. They caught sixty of them with hardly a miss.

Digging a hole, building a fire inside it, waiting for the earth to be sufficiently hot, the fish were then wrapped in peppermint leaves and buried under the coals. The result was the most succulent mountain trout I have ever eaten.

I feel now that I could go on forever describing my life as an Indian in the haunting mountains of northern New Mexico: hunting deer and elk with the men of the pueblo; watching dances wrapped in a blanket while the snow gave the pueblo its fairy tale glow; following the procession on Christmas Eve when the farolitos spilled thick smoke over the pueblo and the men discharged their hunting rifles into the air to honor the Virgin carried on a canopied platform. It would be a little difficult for me to recall all of those living moments because they were a daily succession of learning experiences, pains and joys, all of it threaded with the continuity of belief — nothing done without faith. For me, it was a fairy tale in which hard times were also bountiful.

Cultivating six acres with the help of Mary and the bigger children and occasional help from the family team of horses; being on the road every other month as factory representative visiting a four-state territory, how could it be otherwise; cultivating was not enough, I had to provide for the family too.

With no running water, no electricity, no telephone, only a fireplace and oil stove to warm us during the terrible Taos winters, hard times were many but our cooperation within the family structure, based on trust, love and respect, was total.

Some of my adventures as a *panzaina* (white person in Tiwa) living at the pueblo were funny and I'd like to relate one of them.

Mary was participating in a dance that the pueblos — or even Indians in general — call a public ceremony.

The group of dancers which goes from kiva to kiva around

Mary's grandfather, Juan Concho, patriarch of the family.

the pueblo was by the southern part of the pueblo. I was going to
see them perform and was crossing the huge plaza, full of tourists,
Indians from far away and other visitors. It was a little cold, I
recall, and the breeze from the mountain peaks above the pueblo
was stinging. I had our tiny baby girl, the one we called
Nanpaipapo, Red Sand Flower, well tucked in my blanket. When
wearing such an Indian Blanket, Taos fashion, covering the face to
let only the eyes, nose and mouth be seen, I looked like any
other Indian, my face tanned by the sun. My baby girl's face was
peeping out of the blanket and a *panzaina* lady in her fifties
exclaimed, "Ah! A little white papoose!"

I was infuriated by the indiscretion of the remark and I
retorted, "That's none of your business!" I guess the tourist
woman was surprised I could speak English so well.

Many times I was called squaw man. I didn't mind, I was
proud of it. In the old days, there were trappers and traders who
were called that, too.

Once, attending a banquet in Albuquerque, a drunken
druggist called me squaw man in front of Mary. She left the table
in tears, running to our room in the old Alvarado Hotel. It took

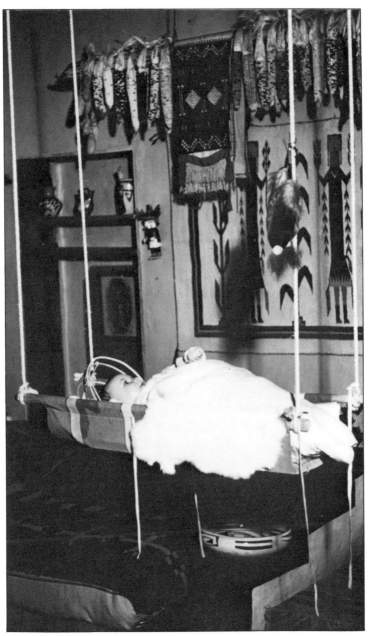

Our daughter, Nanpaipapo, in the Pueblo crib I made for her.

75

the president of the association to calm her down. Mary was irreparably hurt by that incident.

Hunting with my Indian friends and family members was a delight as well as a ceremony. Unlike the white man, in this respect, an Indian will not take an animal's life without asking permission first; asking him to give his life so that a human brother might live. This, of course, like any other action in the Indian world, requires compensation or exchange. This is why a hunter must pray the day before the hunt and perform certain rituals which, in turn, guide the animal into his path.

I can vouch that this relationship between the hunter and the hunted is a working one, because I experienced it myself many times. I do not hunt big game anymore, but when I did, I always performed the necessary rituals to insure the proper order of nature was not disturbed.

After a hunt, we would often sing around a campfire in the mountains at night, roasting deer liver by a creek, singing the old Indian songs. Afterward, I would sleep on the bare ground. Such memories will never leave me, so thankful am I to have been permitted to live such remarkable and vivid moments.

One memory stands out as a monument of Mary's devotion. Sometimes Taos pueblo residents have dances so private no outsider is permitted to attend. One of those was to take place one evening in the main courtyard of the pueblo, after dark. Mary insisted that we go.

No light was permitted either from cars or flashlights. The participants were couples, a huge circle of dancers under Indian blankets which joined each couple as one.

Drummers and singers were in the middle of the dancing circle which contracted at times to form a human vortex around the drummers, then it expanded again, moving out into the darkness.

The night added to the secretiveness of the ceremony and the pulsing motions of dance, heartbeat, drumbeat and night gave me a wonderful sensation of being no longer in the present time, but part of an older, wiser one.

When Wowoka, the Paiute visionary of the late 19th century

described the visions he had of the dance he called the "Ghost Dance," he was talking about the same concentric circle of movement which I experienced that night.

Feasts, dances, ceremonies, community work, baptisms, weddings and funerals succeeded each other in a constant string of events. The best way to describe our life at this time was in a single word — harmony. No life can be overburdened if it is harmonious.

Our little girl, Nanpaipapo, was given a feast at her name-giving ceremony where hundreds of guests from the pueblo and elsewhere came to eat meat, cakes, pies, bread which the women of the pueblo had labored over for days, cooking in the hornos (outdoor mud ovens) which gives a special taste due to the burning of cedar wood. For an entire day guests succeeded guests, sitting on the floor around dishes spread so widely as to cover most of the dining room.

One day I said to Mary, "I too would like an Indian name."

"I will think of the proper one for you," she said, "and I will give it to you in the proper Indian way."

And indeed she did. A few weeks later she said to me, "Let's go to the mountains for a couple of days."

I knew what she meant.

We packed my old army backpack with provisions and sleeping bags and we were en route to the mountains.

Mary, of course, had a special place in mind and it was not long before I found out where it was. The Pueblo of Taos is built at the base of ten to thirteen thousand foot peaks. One of these mountains is called "the spoon." Its southern face, right above the pueblo, is a huge monolith similar to El Capitan of Yosemite Park in California. It is eight or nine miles from the pueblo and its Indian name reminds the people of the old legend of a young Indian maiden who jumped to her death from the top because her lover had been killed.

At the base of the huge mountain, in an almost inextricable jungle of green underbrush, a creek runs between stones, a very wild place.

"Let's follow the creek," Mary said. "It will lead us to the place."

The remainder of the trip was difficult. Almost no one visited this place anymore — at least not often. We had to climb bending under a solid wall of green thorny bushes.

As we drew closer to the huge vertical face of the spoon, from time to time I could see it through the brush and a gentle but persistent noise became more distinct as we approached. I asked Mary about the sound but she would not say anything; her beautiful smile revealed she was determined to keep it a secret to the end.

Tired and with our faces and hands scratched all over, we suddenly emerged into a large opening in the forest at the base of the huge rock. From the height of, perhaps, two or three hundred feet, a trickle of water was falling in an eerie drizzle. It fell into a large pool circled by stones of all colors and shapes.

I was struck by the place, my head bent backward to have a complete view of the waterfall. When I looked at Mary, she was smiling.

Mary and one of our Catcina dolls.

"So, this is the place," I said.

"Yes," she answered.

I was overwhelmed.

I took my clothes off so they wouldn't get soaked but also because the purity of the holy place commanded it.

Mary stripped down to her slip. She had brought the feather of a spotted eagle, a feather she had worn many times when in her buckskin clothes.

Standing together under the waterfall, she let the water fall on the eagle feather, blessing my head and the different parts of my body. I felt strong currents of energy going through my body as she did it.

"Your name will be 'Ghiapateuh,'" she said in a loud voice, "'White Feather!'"

Her head turned toward the sky, her voice addressing the spirit world.

I had never had any doubt that Mary carried within her a distinct and distinctive source of power, strong, compassionate and pervasive. I was convinced that she was using it at that moment of my naming ceremony. She was bringing me to the source of all things in an instant.

We spent the night in the mountains, watching the sky, lying in our sleeping bag close to one another, studying what, one day, would be the immensity of our future home — the myriad of farolitos in the sky.

My life with Red River Flower grew daily. Reaching into my past, I knew that the mystical encounters of my life had prepared me to be receptive to the special teachings of Mary. Her contemporaries at the pueblo, her friends, knew she was someone very special. The only one who didn't seem to know was Mary herself. I had many times had the occasion to witness her resolve, her compassion for other human beings no matter their plight, their race or religion.

Before I came from California to marry her, she took on the incredible task of remodeling the 150-year-old house that her aunt had told us we could live in. She replastered the whole house, whitewashed the inside walls, made a bed supported by adobe walls and even dug outdoor toilets, digging six feet into the rock soil — all, by herself. If that is not an act of love, I don't know of any. As a result of her caring for others, Mary was respected by everyone.

The beautiful sweet white corn I raised, we often sold by the bushel, either to the hospital kitchen run by Catholic sisters or to Spanish residents of Taos, Ranchitos or Ranchos de Taos, and their reaction to Mary was always the same: respect and admiration. Over the years she had generated almost worshipful feelings from people who knew her. She never engendered anything but praise from her Indian fellow men and women, the Spanish people with whom she dealt or the white people whom she knew, worked for or made casual friends with.

Her beauty and poise, no matter what circumstances she found herself in, made people who did not know her want to know her. When we travelled together, heads turned to look at her in the street. When she went on the road with me on one of my business trips, it was embarrassing for her. She was essentially a shy person and people staring made her uncomfortable.

At first I wanted to show my new bride to the world. I was so proud of her but I learned to understand her need for privacy and I respected her feelings. The kind of love relationship we had was based on our acceptance of each other, our knowing the differences we shared.

No wonder throughout these wonderful years, Mary helped me to familiarize myself with so many new aspects of the feminine archetype: Mary, Kwan Yen, Adi-Shakti, Isis and others. I became especially familiar with the different forms taken by the Virgin Mary throughout the centuries. Because I studied what happened in Lourdes, Fatima, Garabandal, Paris and Cairo, I was well prepared to understand Mary's teachings. Through her own devotion, Mary opened for me a new understanding, a new aspect of the same entity: "The Lady of Guadalupe."

I was to learn through her that Indians throughout the Americas have a great devotion for the Indian maiden who appeared on Saturday, December 9, 1531, on the hill of Tepeyac near Mexico City before a Nahuatl Indian going by the Christian name of Juan Diego.

Her real name in Nahuatl, the dialect of the Aztecs, was "Quatl xo Peuh," as she had named herself to Juan Diego.

The whole sequence of events is well known to the religious and scientific community, as well as to the public in general, especially in South and Central America and in the American Southwest.

Because of Mary's own intense devotion to the Virgin who appeared on the outskirts of Mexico City (the ancient Tenochtitlán) on the ruins of the temple of Tonantzin, earth mother of the Aztecs, she brought her into my life, too.

We said many a rosary together at the foot of our bed in front of the Maiden after putting the children to bed for the night. Slowly, I began to experience her presence.

This devotion led to a most extraordinary chain of events which were to influence not only our own lives but also the lives of many other Pueblos in the Rio Grande Valley.

I suppose I may be permitted to say that we started a tradition. This opportunity was given to Mary and me; we did not do anything but accept its guidance.

One time my friend Paul Coze, who now had a rancho in Phoenix, complained to me that the festival he promoted each year under the name of "The Miracle of the Roses," in cooperation with the Scottsdale Chamber of Commerce, was not attracting any Indians.

Although very proud of the fact that the reenactment of the entire Guadalupe mystery had become a popular event there, he was at the same time saddened that the very people for whom the Madonna had come in the first place were not an integral part of the yearly event.

I was touched by his concern. "Paul, I think I can help."

"How?"

"Simple. I will come to the Miracle of the Roses with my family. That will make a dozen Indians right there, including myself," I said with a grin.

Buffalo dancers performing during the celebration.
In background, the mosaic made by Claire Booth Luce.

Paul's face was radiant.

"My God," he said, "I had not thought of that. You would come from New Mexico, several hundred miles away?"

"If it would help!"

"Of course it would help. I'll tell you what. I will ask the Chamber of Commerce to help you with your transportation costs!"

That is how the tradition started.

For several years we attended the Miracle of the Roses and we became the most important part of it. At first, only the Pueblo of Taos participated, but in later years the Pueblos of San Juan, Tesuque, Santo Domingo, Santa Clara and Cochiti sent delegations or dancing groups.

Every year, my Indian friends and fellow pilgrims looked enthusiastically toward filling those Greyhound buses which took us to the land of eternal sun, the Phoenix Valley. They picked oranges out of the trees when their villages were surrounded with snow; that in itself seemed a miracle and contributed to bringing all of us closer to the Madonna.

Paul kept his promise. The Scottsdale Chamber of Commerce helped a great deal with the transportation costs and also found lodging for us. Thanks to Paul's ingenuity, restaurants treated us with sumptuous meals.

I think the greatest of these pilgrimages to honor the Indian world patron saint was in 1954. That year the Pueblo of Taos brought the Matachina dance team in which I myself participated. Santa Clara sent its buffalo and eagle dancers along with its governor. The success of the tradition we started was a miracle in itself as remarked by Mrs. Claire Booth Luce the year she deposited a plaque to commemorate the event. The plaque represented the Indian Madonna which Mrs. Luce made in mosaic.

Those incredible days will stay in my memory forever as the embodiment of faith in the Aztec Maiden who promised succor to her race after the conquest of Mexico by Hernando Cortez.

Many years after Paul Coze's death and Grandpa Concho's departure to the land of his ancestors, the tradition kept on. In Santa Fe it was called the "Pilgrimage of the Mother of the Americas," and took place in 1971. In Espanola, the following year, it was known as the "Mother of the Americas Congress."

It still goes on every year in an Indian kiva somewhere in New Mexico where the originators of the tradition, to honor the little Indian Maiden, meet in the Indian way.

Could she be "White Buffalo Woman" of the Sioux, the Kiowas, the Cheyennes and other Indian tribes? Could she be the one who brought to them the "Calumet of Peace?" Personally, I believe she is, and I also believe that my wife Mary, Red River Flower, was destined to bring us an understanding of this mystery of a native American savior who will never die.

As the peace pipe is circulated among the faithful of all the Indian tribes, from the Dakotas to Hopi, from Mexico to Peru, the Indian Maiden circulates her message of love and compassion for a world ever bent on its own destruction.

83

Because Mary was getting very lonely during my business trips to Utah, Colorado, Arizona and New Mexico every year, I

*Mary and Mrs. Kevama in front of The Lady of Guadalupe
carried in the procession of the Miracle of the Roses in Scottsdale.*

decided to hand in a resignation to my company and look for a job in Santa Fe. I then moved my family to a small house near Canyon Road in Santa Fe, Camino Cerrito, a delightful alley climbing among Spanish adobes and gardens behind Cristo Rey Mission Church.

The financial support I gave my family prompted the move. Taos offered no jobs. As a loving wife and mother, Mary agreed to the move, but I could soon see the severance from the daily contact with her people and her ancestral home was making her very sad.

The umbilical cord that unites Indians with the collective soul of their people is strong and, in Mary's case, the fragility of this tie may have been damaged by the move. Yet there was nothing she or I could do about it.

I often wonder if the cultures which have separated Indian tribes from each other, and have exiled them from their mother land, have ever realized their crime is against Mother Nature, a crime that might weigh a great deal in the balance of all our futures.

Today, in Brazil, Ecuador, Paraguay and other South American countries from one side of the continent to the other, the same crime is being perpetuated every day. Indians are being treated like substandard human groups. Their beliefs, religions, social structures are violated, their God-given rights denied.

When will the invaders recognize the Indians' right to exist as nations? When will the so-called superior cultures and the ever-present industrial and technological powers hear the message of White Buffalo Woman and the Indian Maiden, Quatl xo Peuh? After four hundred years of being trampled on, the Indian is still with us. Some have gone like the buffalo, others come back in great numbers, also like the buffalo. When will the white man see the sustaining faith which has kept the Indian alive after so many massacres? When will he realize the unified blessing of being one with the land and its people?

To help meet the necessities of everyday living in a big town, Mary and I established a small business, a small trading post. We had found a tiny shop to rent in one of the landmarks of old Santa Fe. Like so many others, it is now obliterated by expanding businesses. Burro Alley it was called.

It was a small placita, now taken over by the Palace Restaurant. In those days, it was a charming spot, full of old New Mexico atmosphere. The Shed occupied one side of the little courtyard; we, a shoe repair shop and a couple of other small shops occupied the rest.

Going to Gallup to buy the Indian trading goods we needed to open the shop was great fun. Mary knew several of the traders from her days at Zuni. We brought back Catcina dolls, Navajo rugs, Zuni turquoise jewelry, most of it on consignment, the trading custom of the day since small traders started their businesses without much capital. We started without any.

Uncle Pete and his wife Isabel Concha built Mary an adobe Indian oven in front of the shop. As far as I know, Mary was the first of her people to bake Indian bread and pies to sell to the public. Every day at noon a long line of customers would be waiting for the hot breads and pies to come out of the oven.

As far as we were concerned life could have stayed the way it was. We were very content. Although transplanted from the sheltered Pueblo communal life where everyone is a friend or relative, Mary and the children had adjusted quite well to the new situation. Many a weekend saw us packing up and going back home to the pueblo. But destiny, this overseer of human life, sometimes has plans of its own, plans derived from a more wholistic view of each of us, rather than the linear one that is our own perception.

For quite some time Mary had suffered from the symptoms of a goiter. Her neck began to enlarge considerably. I would say to her: "Mary, we have to see a doctor. The removal of a goiter is not complicated and you are much too beautiful to endure this needless swelling." But she was unconvinced. Surgery was frightening to her, as it is to everyone, although for an Indian to have the body violated from its pristine God-given state, is a sacrilege.

Finally, and reluctantly, she agreed to have the operation and she was operated on at the Bernalillo County Indian Hospital (now the University of New Mexico Medical School Hospital) in Albuquerque. The surgery was a success, but a week later I had to take her back because her body ached with chills. I had to leave her in a crowded ward to go back to Santa Fe to take care of our four children. Three days later I cam back to see her and discovered that Mary was on the critical list and in an oxygen tent. No one had contacted me.

EPILOGUE

On August 23, 1959, Mary died of the dreaded staphylococcus, ten days after the small goiter had been successfully removed from her neck. She was killed by the deadly virus that infected many hospitals in the nation at that time.

A few days after the dreadful event, looking for papers in the drawer of her little desk, I found the poem at the end of this book written in her handwriting. She had been working on it before she left for the hospital. It was unfinished; death interrupted its completion. When I read it, I was overcome by the feeling that Mary knew of her death.

Standing by her hospital bed, her hand gently curled into mine, only minutes before she left this earth, she could not talk any more but could hear me. Overcome by grief and desolation, I said to her, "Mary, my sweet love...can you hear me?"

She indicated by a sign of her head that she did. I put my head close to hers.

"You are leaving us," I said, tears burning my eyes, "but where ever you are going to be, please do not abandon us... keep in touch..."

She motioned that she would.

Looking deep into my eyes for the last time, Red River Flower peacefully let her spirit float away...she was going home.

In many ways, she kept her promise. She spoke to me through music that was privately known to us.

I could not have known what I asked of her would lead to communications beyond the bondage of life and death. But it absolutely did.

Years have passed now, and Mary is still as close to my heart as the day I held her hand at the moment of her death.

I am glad I asked what I did.

Red River Flower is resting in the little cemetery of the Taos Pueblo, among her people. Taos Pueblo buries its dead in the ruins of their old church. Destroyed by the advancing troops of General Kearny on February 3, 1847, when both Indians and Mexicans took refuge in it in hopes of defending the village, only to succumb under American artillery.

My arms wrapped around her body as the Taos Pueblo ambulance brought her back home, I remembered what happened in the Cristo Rey Church perhaps only a month before her death.

Alone in the beautiful mission church on Canyon Road, only a stone's throw from our house, we were praying one afternoon. Mary was very private and shy among people she did not know, so she always wanted to go to church when nobody was there.

Our silent prayer and meditation over, she bent her head slightly, indicating she wanted to tell me something. I notice that her face was illuminated with a very unusual glow.

"Have you seen this lady sitting in front of us?" Mary asked in a whisper.

I was astounded because no one else was in the church.

"She never turns her head," she said. "She wears a white dress without a shawl, her hair long and neatly combed and trimmed at her shoulders; a diadem of twelve stars on her head."

And now that my head was touching her rigid body, my face streaming with tears as the ambulance sped away toward Taos, I realized who the lady was...She had come to show Mary the way, delivering her from life on earth, opening the unlimited horizons of the spirit that we once perceived the night after she gave me my Indian name, gazing at the firmament.

Indian funerals are long and painful in their cruel simplicity. Mary's lasted four days altogether.

Wrapped in as many as twelve blankets, my own on top of the others, she lay on the bare adobe floor of our old Grandpa's home in the pueblo.

Day and night, most of the pueblo residents came to pray, say the rosary and bless her with tears.

In the hearts of her own people, Red River Flower was no ordinary Indian. She was a symbol of their pride and strength, personal grace and beauty remembered in hundreds of candles lighted all around her body during the wake.

What an awakening to the most painful reality of my life, alone now and grieving. Mary was gone but somehow I knew Red River Flower would survive.

On the fourth day early in the morning, the close relatives had to dip in the Taos River, naked. The freezing waters rushing out of Blue Lake on my naked body made the myth of emergence all the more real.

I thought a great deal about how Red River Flower entered my life and how she had left it. She had been the messenger of good tidings. But more than that, she led me to certain dimensions of the human soul I would never have known without her.

From the first moment when France, my little girl of ten, then, led me to her, through a blissful married life, ending with the transcendence pact which bound us beyond life and death, there could be no mistake — Mary had been sent to me.

I had been prepared for this, my coming to America, Paul Coze, Hopi and finally, Taos. All the introduction I needed to be introduced to the message of White Buffalo Woman and Quatl xo Peuh.

This longing for Indian values that was present in me since childhood made so much sense now. The message had been clear to the end as Mary's departure indicated to me the grief was over: I was finally ready to accept the spiritual responsibilities which go with revelation.

"The word Virgo is a corruption of the root word for mother in the primitive languages of the world.

"The Virgin was the founder of the Matriarchate which then dominated civilization.

"The myths and legends around Lillith and the Amazon Queen defeated by Hercules are allegories teaching the emergence of the Spiritual Man from the control of Mother under the Sign of Virgo.

"Eve, Isis and Mary brought the Christ child from the mental to the emotional, then to the physical plane.

"Virgo is the valley of deep experience, slow, gentle but powerful crisis and is the womb of time."

So astrology tells us.

Hera was known to the Greeks, Juno to the Romans, Kwan Yen to the Orient, Adi Shakti to India, the Black Madonna to Poland, Piemont and Sicily, Isis to ancient Egypt, Wisdom to the

Jews, Mary to the Christians.

I had to meet the archetype who would bridge the Christian world and the American Indian and I did it with Red River Flower who brought me to the Lady of Guadalupe.

White Buffalo Woman said to the Oglala Sioux, "Tell your people that I am coming. A big tepee should be built for me in the center of the nation." And, Quatl xo Peuh said to Juan Diego, "Go and tell the bishop of Mexico City that a temple should be built here for me so I can give all my love, my compassion, my help and my protection to the people. I am the merciful mother of all of you who live united in this land, and of all mankind, of all those who love me, of those who cry to me, of those who seek me, of those who have confidence in me. Here I will hear their weeping, their sorrow, and will remedy and alleviate all their multiple sufferings, necessities and misfortunes." (Exact translation from Nahuatl into English from the text of Juan Diego's account in 1531.)

The Aztec nation had been defeated nineteen years before at the hand of the Spanish conquistador Hernando Cortez. Left without a culture, a leader, a national entity, a religion or even an identity, Quatl xo Peuh's message delivered on the very spot where the Temple of Tonantzin, Earth Mother of the Aztecs, once stood, was bound to reach deep into the Indian soul.

The temple she asked for now reconstructed, millions of Indians, Mexicans and people from all over the world visit the Indian holy maiden every year, fulfilling her prophecy to care and give solace to whomever believes in her powers.

I went to visit her a few years ago on the hill of Tepeyac at the very edge of the lake which once surrounded Tenochtitlán, capital of the Aztec empire, and I fulfilled a promise I made to her years before.

I can vouch for the fact that the Indians do not forget her. I can also say with absolute certitude that she will never forget them, either.

STEP BY STEP

The spirit has not left
Each step harder to Thee
Within me it is kept
as if to climb a tree.

Surely to grow, a tree
needs water and food
My Lord to get nearer to Thee,
give me body and blood.

Like a bird I'd fly,
If I had wings.
With no strength,
I cannot try.

Still my spirit has wings
My love for thee,
I know what it brings.

If I were to choose,
From millions of flowers
And did not know.
If I were to lose.

Upon your... *

* Unfinished poem found in Mary's desk at the shop.

POSTSCRIPT

For a very long time guilt over loaded my memories of Mary.

What if I had not convinced her to be operated on...If I had not taken her to the Indian Hospital but to St. Vincent Hospital instead!...If I had not left her alone at the hospital...

Would she be alive today?

But what about the poem and the beautiful lady sitting in front of us in the Church?!

I know now that, although in a much different dimension, Mary still lives.

Our song, a familiar scent, let me know from time to time that she kept her promise.

It might indeed sound strange to some but deep within myself I know that she reveals her presence at times. Not just the desire for it to be so, but a very concrete feeling that she is next to me.

I have entertained the thought at times that she might come back in physical form somewhere, someday. But I would rather think that she has accomplished the full cycle of her spirit life and that she found peace, eternal peace and that the being she once saw in the Cristo Rey Church in Santa Fe was the herald, the messenger that led her to this place where contentment is no longer a wish but an absolute reality.